Advanced Figure
Modelling

THE ESSENTIAL REFERENCE FOR THE FIGURE MODELLER

Vol. I

PERISCOPIO PUBLICATIONS

CONTRIBUTORS
Natalya Alekseeva - Pietro Balloni
Mike Blank - Alain De Busse
Natalya Charushina - Davide Decina
Marcus Eckmann - Ray Farrugia
Jaume Ortiz Forns - Christos Katselos
Stephen Mallia - Grigoris Marmatakis
Jurgen Nirschl - Christos Panayotopoulos
Christos Panayotou - Costas Rodopoulos
Diego Ruina - Christos Stamatopoulos
Babis Stathis - Panayotis Tsetsekas
Paris Tsirchoglou

EDITOR
Stelios Demiras

TRANSLATORS
Thanos Mentzelopoulos,
Costas Rodopoulos

PROOF EDITORS
Charles Davis, Ken Jones

UNIFORM RESEARCH AND RECONSTRUCTION
Christos Giannopoulos

ART DIRECTOR AND COVER DESIGN
Dimitra Mitsou

ADVANCED FIGURE MODELLING Vol. 1
First published in Greece in 2008
by Periscopio Publications

8, G. Seferi Str., 17234, Dafni, Greece.
E-mail: info@periscopio.gr
www.periscopio.gr

All rights reserved. Reproduction in part or in whole is forbidden without prior written permission from the publisher, except in case of brief quotations used in reviews.

ISBN: 978-960-6740-49-7

Contents

6	The Infantry of Median Wars, 490 B.C. - 480 B.C. (History)
18	Thermopylae 480 B.C. - 54 mm
32	Spartan Officer, Battle of Thermopylae - 150 mm
34	Greek Hoplite - 54 mm
36	Greek "Siceliota" - 54 mm
38	Alexander the Great, King of the World - 90 mm
42	Mongol Warrior, A Scratchbuilt figure - 60 mm
44	Painting Faces with Acrylic Colors - 90 mm
46	Mameluk - 90 mm
56	Germanic Warrior - 75 mm
60	Praefectus Classis, I-II century A.D. A Roman Naval Officer - 75 mm
64	Praetorian Centurion - 75 mm
70	Attila and the Black Huns' Empire (History)
75	Templar Sergeant XIII Century, The Villain - 90 mm
78	Byzantine Imperial Cavalry Standard-bearer - 75 mm (13th-14th century A.D.)
92	Italian Knight in White Armor, 1440-1450 - 90 mm
96	Ivan the Terrible - 90 mm
102	Scratchbuilt Mounted Russian Knight - 120 mm Three vignettes centered on the same subject (14th century A.D.)
106	Viking Warrior, A Scratchbuilt Figure - 54 mm
109	The Teutonic Knights of the 13th century The Crusaders from Germany - 54 mm
116	Viking Hersir, The Tall Warrior - 90 mm
120	The Warrior of the East, Ashigaru, Japanese foot arquebusier Azuchi momoyama period (1568-1600) - 90 mm
126	"The Lost Documents" - 75 mm How to sculpt 75 mm figures for comercial casting
139	Scottish Officer of 42nd Regiment, Officer of Black Watch - 54 mm
144	Pirate Madagascar 1720 - 150 mm
146	19th Century Bersaglieri Officer The Italian Army's "fighting cocks" - 54 mm
148	Chasseur of the Imperial Guard The Emperor's Bodyguards - 54 mm
152	Louisiana Tigers - 54 mm
154	French Cuirassier 1812-1815 The "Heavy Armor" of the French Army - 90 mm
163	SS Standartenführer - 200 mm
166	SS Panzergrenadier 1945, Painting Italian camouflage - 50 mm (1/35)
172	2nd Ranger Battalion, Omaha Beach, Normandy, 6th June 1944 - 54 mm
174	SS Sturmbanführer of Artillery The Officer who watched the Panzer pass by... - 90 mm

Preface

While, in its present form, the hobby of modelling might be relatively new, the ambition of recreating real life in miniature is really very ancient. Today, many hobby enthusiasts engaged in making and/or painting miniatures (or figures, if you prefer), tend to say that the miniature is an art form, divorced from any other area of modelling. It is not easy to disagree as, in recent years, miniature scenes of unbelievable beauty and technical expertise have appeared. Replicating humans in miniature form is always more attractive than, say, just making vehicles, armor, or other modelling subjects. The small scenes that take shape under the artist's hands are of an exceptional intricacy and demand large amounts of effort, as well as great a deal of time. However, the creators of such scenes never regret the time and effort involved as the end result is enchanting and awe inspiring for everyone to see.

In this book, that has taken many months in preparation, we tried to gather representative samples as well as different forms of work. Here you will find the painting of commercial pieces, sculpting, conversions, work on ground presentation and scenery, historical texts, indeed, many different aspects of our hobby have been covered. However, we have also endeavored to ensure they are all the same standard, from creators and painters from all corners of the globe, to make this presentation as interesting as possible for the modeller, be they beginner or master.

This collection of work is aimed at all levels of modellers. Color tone recipes, sculpting tips, brushwork tricks, groundwork techniques, and much more, all submitted by well known artists, compile this mosaic of inspiration that we hope will keep you occupied for many happy hours.

Depending on the success of this first book and its enthusiastic acceptance by the modelling world, we would be more than happy to try even harder on a future second edition, featuring yet more of the endless stream of material that these brilliant creators can offer.

And so, we deliver this book to you, knowing that a high level of your pleasure will be the proof of our success.

The Editor
Stelios Demiras

Special Thanks
A large book of this nature without special thanks would be like oil paint without turpentine, so ...here we go. Our thanks go in advance to all those artists who are sharing their work with you in this book, but especially to Charles Davis, Ken Jones, Luca Marchetti, Pietro Balloni, Diego Ruina and Costas Rodopoulos. They have all inspired us with great ideas, technical assistance and full support throughout the long gestation period of the book.

The Infantry of Median Wars (490-480 B.C.)

Text - historical presentation - illustration and original representation of uniforms: Christos Giannopoulos

This particular article, and the colored illustrations that accompany it, aim to present a concise but comprehensive presentation of the land forces of Greece and Persia at the onset of the Median Wars, according to confirmed archaeological material from Greece, Italy, Asia Minor, India and Iran. The study focuses strictly on the infantry costumes of the two protagonists, but does not attempt to present the cavalry, the navy or any other army corps from the particular period, neither does it, of course, constitute a complete academic thesis of the Median Wars.

During the first decades of 5th century B.C., Greece was divided into many small states, which fought between themselves for control of the country's vital resources within the framework of one strange ritual: every able-bodied citizen of each belligerent city-state, armed with helmet, round shield, cuirass, greaves, spears, and swords, made up the compact formations and clashed at a predetermined locality, which was sited a safe distance from the non-belligerent population.

It was the age of Hoplite Phalanx and the chivalrous ferocity that characterized this obscure and, for some, primitive style of warfare. The significance of a catholic war that included the destruction of homes, clearance of cultivated fields, slaughter of domestic animals, and brutality against non-belligerent citizens, was unthinkable in the Greece of the 7th to 5th century B.C.. The whole ferocity of war was defused in just a few acres of ground between pre-determined armed clans that wished to resolve the disagreement between their cities immediately and then return to their families or ensure their survival through self-sacrifice.

The hoplites wore helmets that covered a large part of their faces and altered their physiognomy, giving them the aspect of "alien" beings. Large round shields (called "hoplon," from where the word "hoplite" originates) were adorned with colourful representations of animals, demons or fabulous monsters that were conceptually connected with warfare, courage, faith in certain ideal or even the fates that wove the thread of someone's life. Certain symbols were popular in particular regions (the head of Medusa represented the Spartans and their settlements in Italy), other were related with the legends of a particular city (the white bull of Marathon was the symbol of Athens), while symbols, common to the whole Greek nation represented bravery (the lion for example) or good luck (the swastinx and the three-leg). Some shields had peculiar forms (the Boeotian body shield that covered adjacent notches and reminds us of the octagonal Mycenean shield), while other had metal bosses in the form of animals, or covered the outer surfaces with metal scales.

The cuirasses of the Greek warriors were manufactured from bronze and were often embossed with the rudimentary muscular proportions of the male torso while at the same time they possessed a residual collar (remnant of earlier times). The metal cuirasses hat were developed after the Median Wars revealed wonderful muscular thoraxes that constituted real works of art. The lighter cuirasses used in Greece were of a complex manufacture, compiled from multiple layers of linen or leather that were sometimes was overlaid with metal scales. The advantage of the composite cuirass (linothoraxes) was that it allowed better mobility and flexibility (the bearer could bend or kneel comfortably behind his shield) but, obviously, offered decreased protection against spear or sword thrusts. The composite cuirasses also introduced metal laminae, although these were easily corrupted where each scale was sewn to the next one when they were struck a slashing blow from a sword. Even if some Hoplite armies remained faithful in the use of the metal cuirass (the Spartans, for example) there are some cases, like that of the Athenians that used exclusively the light linen thorax at the Battle of Marathon. It enabled to charge at a progressively increased speed under heavy arrow "storm," of the Persian army.

The spectacle of the charge of a Hoplite column was, according to Xenofon, terrifying: a compact wall

LEONIDAS. *A hypothetical representation of the heroic king based on the famous statue in the Sparta Museum. This is considered to be a portrayal of Leonidas (a view questioned in recent years). There are no distinctive uniform features setting him apart from a mere hoplite -a normal situation in a society where all men were lifetime warriors of the front line. The king's Corinthian helmet is based on that found on the statue, and features unusual cheek guards in the form of a ram's head. Horned animals did not only symbolize bravery in battle, but also indicated an aristocratic warrior's descent from a god. Leonidas was considered a descendant of the demigod Hercules and, therefore, of Zeus, father of the gods. His shield is decorated with the head of Gorgo, the female demon, whose terrifying glance turned her enemies into stone. The impressive figure of Gorgo often appears on Spartan shields and symbolized the aggressive spirit and qualities of leadership of Spartan women. Leonidas' dynamic wife was named Gorgo, a name which would be considered offensive in other Greek city-states. (uniform research and reconstruction by Christos Giannopoulos)*

A SPARTAN HOPLITE. *There was a certain uniformity in Spartan battle dress during the Persian Wars. All hoplites wore red clothing and a bronze, bell-shaped cuirass. Linen armored cuirasses had not yet become universally popular. They also wore greaves, carried a hoplon shield and wore a closed Corinthian helmet. Particular differences could be spotted on shield emblems (which were related to certain units or "morai") by the shape of the crest holder or the decorative patterns woven on the soldier's tunics. (uniform research and reconstruction by Christos Giannopoulos)*

of shields covered with strange symbols, behind which raised up alien helmets with palpitating plumes. A spear "forest" was progressively lowered in front of the formation, forewarning any opponents of the massacre that would follow.

As the rival formations approached, the trot accelerated, and the martial cry of the ancient Greeks, "Elelelelei," filled the air like the hysterical sound of thousands of buzzards, thirsty for blood, in an ultimate effort to "break" the opponent's morale. The warriors' closed helmets limited both their hearing ability and their peripheral sight. Each front line combatant advanced, able only to look ahead, looking around the shield's frame and hoping that the men on both sides were still alive and covering him from with their own shields. If a comrade was struck down, this meant that, in just a few moments, he would be thinly engulfed in a hostile crowd, with visibility that was limited to one metre by the crowd, the dust, the splintering of wood-shafted spears falling from all sides and the sunlight reflecting from the enemy shields. This clash of column versus column experienced by the Greek armies, although a nightmarish scenario, proved to be the decisive point of their supremacy against the nationally heterogeneous hordes of the Achemenid Persians. The Athenians and Spartans were active members of a society that spontaneously invested in them, and profoundly believed in the regime and their homelands' way of life.

It would, however, be unfair to underestimate the martial machine of the dynasty Achemenid, a dynasty that controlled populations across three continents. In contrast to politically divided Greece, the Persian Empire of the 5th century B.C. was a huge bureaucratic organism, that delegated (ostensibly at least) the powerful central authority, but also had the disadvantage of centrifugal tendencies from the coexistence of different speaking populations, under the ever watchful eye and the whip of the most capable Iranian dignitaries that undermined each other in the constant pursuit of favour in the palace hierarchy or ascendance to the pinnacle of power.

The hard core of the Persian' infantry were the indigenous Iranians that fought in decuries (Datha) of archers, commanded by an NCO lancer with a human sized shield (sparabara) and, in the rear by another NCO with a whip (pascadathapatis) that kept the formation from collapse (the equivalent of the Roman Optio). All the native Iranians were armed, besides the bow, with a short sword (akinaka) that was to the right thigh and the characteristic Iranian axe ("Sagaris"), that was able, due to its cuneiform beak, to penetrate every type of Greek helmet and all kinds of cuirasses.

The Persian cuirasses were manufactured from leather or layered linen that, in the case of elite infantry units (for example the Immortals) was covered with metal scales. The officers' breastplates had gilded scaling and were also decorated with solar disks. Unfortunately, it is impossible to say with certainty, in what degree the armour was used within the Persian infantry, as the ancient Greek vases portray the Persian foot soldiers sometimes with armor while, in other cases, with simple, cloth uniforms. The off-hand statistics, estimated from these vases, give the impression that 60% of the Persian infantry entered into battle without any armor and were supported by the heavy "fire" of archers. (The arrows would exhaust the opponents before the final clash and the prolific numerical advantage held by the Persian army as a whole, would discourage any further resistance). Another disadvantage of the Persian infantry was the limited use of the helmet and, of course, shields (remember, only the Sparabara Decuries leaders carried a shield) that rendered them vulnerable in frontal attack against the compact shielded mass of Greek soldiers. It appears that the Persian Kings lived with the continuous fear of revolt and left the majority of their inhabitants, and also complementary infantry poorly equipped, so that the faithful imperial units of the "Immortals" would easily guide it.

United Persian decuries constituted the Achemenic division, "Baivarabam," of ten thousand men that walked into battle disciplined to the blowing of trumpets and guided by standard-bearers (the use of flags and banners was a Persian military innovation previously unknown in ancient Greece). It is worth mentioning, that one, and only Imperial division were numerically equivalent and often superior to any possible army from a Greek city-state. All the divisions of indigenous Iranians were numerically equivalent to the total combatants that Greece could call to arms, that is to say, roughly 100,000 soldiers. If we take into consideration, that the Persian indigenous infantry divisions were strengthened during each expedition by an equal number of reserves of infantry from the conquered populations of Asia and northern Africa, it is easily understood that the volume of the Great King's army doubled in size and considerably faced down any prospect of a constituted resistance. Herodotus states (certainly with patriotic exaggeration) that it was an invasion force of millions, including slaves, prostitutes and captives, swallowing rivers in its path or erasing entire cities from the map with each raid.

The Seil figure in 54 mm "Greek Thespian Hoplite in Thermopylae" (SH54034) based on the original illustration of Christos Giannopoulos. Sculpting: Yury Serevryakov, figure painting: Kim Man Jin. This figure was awarded as the Model of the Year 2006 from the German magazine Kit Figure-Modell-Journal.

The Romeo Models figure in 54 mm "Lokros Hoplite" (RM 54-62) based on the original illustration of Christos Giannopoulos. Sculpting: Maurizio Bruno, figure painting: Danillo Cartacci.

A BLACK-CLAD THESPIAN.
The warrior illustrated here is representative of the 700 Thespians who fought to the last man at Thermopylae. During the 5th century B.C., the emblem of the city of the Thespians was the half moon of Black Aphrodite on a Boetian shield. The worship of life-giving force, represented by Aphrodite and Eros, was a central theme in Thespian religious belief. Each piece of this Thespian warrior's armor is in the color of mourning and darkness and shows his belief that he will march into a battle never to return. (uniform research and reconstruction by Christos Giannopoulos)

A WARRIOR FROM MAINLAND GREECE.
The artwork captures the general image of the Locrian and Phocian soldiers who fought alongside the Spartans at Thermopylae. The warrior illustrated wears an archaic Corinthian helmet with impressive double crest holders (the red-figure pottery of the time also shows helmets with triple crest holders). His cuirass is made of flexible composite materials covered with metal scales on the outer surface. He wears bronze leg armor, and carries a large "hoplon-type" sword. The very archaic decorative designs on the shield show a continual spiral pattern (a symbol of fire), a right-handed swastika (a symbol of the unconquerable) and a four-spoke wheel (a symbol of the War God's chariot). (uniform research and reconstruction by Christos Giannopoulos)

A PHRYGIAN SWORD-BEARING PELTAST (TAKABARA). The Thracians of Asia, who lived in the hilly regions of western Anatolia (Phrygians, Armenians, Cappadocians, Cilicians, Bithynians, etc.), were used as auxiliary infantry and often as an auxiliary marine force. The Phrygian warrior in the illustration is equipped in the usual fashion of his nation: a leather hat with side wings, a long mantle, garments decorated with geometrical patterns, leather greaves, a pelt-type shield (taka in Persian). He also carries javelins and grasps an Iranian-style curved, slashing sword. (uniform research and reconstruction by Christos Giannopoulos)

ATHENIAN MARINE. The only surviving color depiction of an Athenian marine comes from a wall fresco at the Elmeli funerary monument in Asia Minor. This 5th century fresco in combination with contemporary red figure pottery provided the evidence for this illustration. The majority of the Athenian hoplites and marines appear to have worn composite cuirass armor made of white linen and leather decorated with red piping. The Athenian marine at Elmeli is shown wearing a Corinthian helmet with a red and white crest and a blue tunic. The single-edged broadsword and the shield emblem are based on red figure pottery showing the Athenians fighting the Persians. (uniform research and reconstruction by Christos Giannopoulos)

A KISSIAN SHIELD BEARER SECTION LEADER (SPARABARA-PASCHADATHAPATIS). The Kissians were considered descendants of the Elamites, a pre-Iranian race from the Persian Gulf, and, according to Herodotus, they were among the first to attack the Spartans at the Thermopylae pass. The section leader illustrated here is clad in typical Median fashion. His clothing includes a long-sleeved tunic and trousers featuring woven Eurasian patterns. His defensive armament consists of a large, spara-type composite shield and a padded linen cuirass that, according to Herodotus, resembled fish scales. His offensive weapons include a short spear and a short double-edged sword (akinakes), the latter suspended from his belt and tied to the right thigh. Herodotus writes that "the clothing of the Kissians was similar to the Persians," but on their heads, instead of soft caps, they wore turbans. (uniform research and reconstruction by Christos Giannopoulos)

PERSIAN DECURION WITH SHIELD (SPARABARA) 500-490 B.C. The sparabara made up the shielded first line of Persian infantry defence. They provided protection for the archers in the rear as these began to loose a rain of arrows on the advancing enemy. His complex dress and shield (of cane and skin) are decorated with linear Eurasian patterns. These patterns were indicative of the geographic regions were they were recruited. Their offensive arms consisted of a strong spear with a round metal base and the characteristic Iranian dagger, akinaka. His body was protected by a quilted linen cuirass that incorporated leather flaps, known to the ancient Greeks as "pteruges" (wings). (uniform research and reconstruction by Christos Giannopoulos)

A "KUSHIYA" ETHIOPIAN AUXILIARY FOOT SOLDIER. According to Herodotus, these Ethiopians from the kingdom of Kush were clad in leopard or lion skins and painted one half of their body dark red and the other half white. Though the ancient historians refer to them as archers, on many red figure vases they are shown fighting as light infantry or marines armed with spiked clubs and pelta shield. (uniform research and reconstruction by Christos Giannopoulos)

LYKIAN MARINE IN PERSIAN ARMY SERVICE (489-479 B.C.). The warriors of Asia Minor wore armor influenced by the Greeks. However, certain items such as the elaborate shield, the convex sword of type "drepanon" (reaping hook), and the forked spear remain local peculiarities. (uniform research and reconstruction by Christos Giannopoulos)

SATRAP MERCENARY OF HALYBIAN NATION (500-400 B.C.). Xenofon characterizes the Halybians as among of the bravest yet wilder populations, that lived in the Persian empire of the Achemenids. They wore helmets and greaves, tufted linen cuirasses with rope hangings and carried convex machetes or long spears with lengths of six metres (a precocious form of sarissa spear). In front of their enemies they performed wild war dances, and attacked with screaming fury carrying the severe heads of fallen enemies. (uniform research and reconstruction by Christos Giannopoulos)

ATHENIAN MARINE (489-479 B.C.).
The young warrior in the illustration wears the characteristic armament of the Athenian marines during the later period of the Median Wars: The "Attic" helmet with over painted skull and white/ red plume, a refined composite cuirass with added protection from bronze tiles and scales, bronze greaves, a round shield, a conventional thrusting spear and the classic hoplite sword, but of mediocre size. As noted, the blue of his tunic as well as the red and white decoration on some items of his equipment (helmet plume, leather cuirass flaps, shoulder guards and sword scabbard) are supported by archaeological evidence. (uniform research and reconstruction by Christos Giannopoulos)

AN ATHENIAN HOPLITE, 490 B.C. This particular warrior represents a typical Athenian hoplite from the lower classes that fought at Marathon. He wears an Attican-style crested helmet, light leather wings, long bronze greaves, and is carrying a "hoplon" type shield, the face of which has a woolen cloth attached to protect the legs from Persian arrows (some infantrymen used leather aprons for the same purpose). His offensive weapons are the long thrusting spear and the thrusting-slashing sword (not shown here). (uniform research and reconstruction by Christos Giannopoulos)

A PERSIAN, OR MEDIAN HIGH-RANKING OFFICER, 5th CENTURY B.C. The illustrated polemarch wears luxurious armor made of gold plated scales and decorated with sun disks, a fact that brings to mind the phrase in ancient Greek literature of the "golden-clad Medes." All items of his outfit (cloth tiara tied under his chin, long-sleeved tunic, wide breeches with purple strips, leather boots and large arrow case containing both the bow and its arrows) is indicative of the pure Medic culture, while his golden decorations (around the neck and wrists) reveal that he is a man of a high social standing who was part of the King's entourage. His offensive weapons are the bow, the long slashing sword, the short akinakes sword, and the Iranian wedge-shaped ax known as a "sagaris." (uniform research and reconstruction by Christos Giannopoulos)

INDIAN ARCHERS (500-330 B.C.). *The Indians accompanied the Persians in their expeditions almost as independent allies and not as a conquered people. They were better cavalrymen than infantry, although the Persians used them primarily as complementary archers. They carried enormous bows made of bamboo, capable of penetrating all types of armor at short distances. The Indians swords were large, two-handed ones. (uniforms research and reconstruction by Christos Giannopoulos)*

A PLATAEAN WARRIOR, 500-490 B.C. This particular illustration is based on depictions of warriors on items of pottery excavated from the Plateaens' tomb at Marathon. It appears that most Plataean warriors were aged between 15 and 25, and, strangely, are depicted wearing long mantles when they fought. They wore undecorated Corinthian helmets, long bronze greaves, and carried shields of the "hoplon" or Boeotian "thyreos" types (these can also be seen on some of depictions of Athenian hoplites of the period). (uniform research and reconstruction by Christos Giannopoulos)

ATHENIAN WARLORD, 490 B.C. The composite cuirasses of wealthy, noble class citizens of Athens were covered with overlapping bronze scales, while the fringes were decorated with colourful patterns. The officer's Corinthian helmet is bicolored, with the skull in the colour of bronze and the face protector dyed black to make it more impressive. The helmet's raised crest holder, exaggerates the warlord's stature, while the metal covering on his shield is decorated with the white bull's head, a popular emblem among the warriors of Marathon (recalling the battle of the hero Thiseas against the giant white bull of Marathon). (uniform research and reconstruction by Christos Giannopoulos)

A FULLY ARMED "IMMORTAL."
He is armed with a spear with a butt in the shape of an apple, a short sword of the akinakes type, a bow and arrows and a lushly decorated large shield known as "spara." He wears a rich scaled cuirass over his colorful garments. Instead of a helmet, he wears a classic Persian tiara, which was not very protective. (uniform research and reconstruction by Christos Giannopoulos)

AN ELITE SACA ARCHER,
500 - 480 B.C. The Saca archers were the elite allied units of the Empire's infantry, the equivalent of the Roman "auxilia" units. They were particularly capable and could even fight as shock troops. Apart from their bow, they were also equipped with other offensive weapons, including a curved sword and the wedge-shaped "sagaris" ax, which could penetrate all types of Greek helmet and cuirasses. The Sacas' uniform's national identity was the leopard-skin cap with its pointed top from which some of their tribal names were derived, such as "Saca Tigrakhauda," meaning "the Sacas with the pointed caps." In the ancient world it was strongly rumored that their clothing and padded cuirasses were made from human skin. (uniform research and reconstruction by Christos Giannopoulos)

Thermopylae 480 B.C.

The thousands of years of Greek history offer the modeller a wide variety of themes and ideas. This is especially so in the 54 mm scale where most companies have released a rich collection of Greek figures. The modeller's choices appear endless if combined with easily carried out conversions. In this article, I will present my version of the Battle of Thermopylae, using Andrea's excellent kit of the "Spartan's Last Stand" as a starting point.

GRIGORIS MARMATAKIS

54 mm
Spartan's Last Stand (480 B.C.): Andrea Miniatures (SG-S06)
Greek Hoplite 5th c B.C.: Pegaso Models (54-180)
Hoplita de Ampurias: El Viejo Dragon (CG 03)
Victorious Celt: Verlinden Productions (1798)
Wounded Macedonian: El Viejo Dragon (CG 117)
Preiser figures 1/32

Acrylic colours: Vallejo, Andrea
Oil paints: Winsor & Newton
Epoxy putty: Andrea, Duro, Magic Sculp
Acrylic paste for constructing the groundwork: Vallejo
Printers' inks: gold, silver
Gloss varnish: Humbrol
Red acrylic ink: Citadel

The final moments of the Greek hoplites on the hill of Colonus, as seen by an observer. They fell to the last man under the onslaught of a rain of Persian arrows. A little earlier, at dawn of the final day of the Battle at Thermopylae, those who were still able to stand and fight arrayed in the open field and not in an enclosed area, knowing that they faced death.

HISTORIC DATA

King Darius died in 486 B.C. with his dream of conquering Greece unfulfilled. His son and heir, Xerxes, undertook this mission after his father's death. In 480 B.C., after gathering a huge army of 200,000 infantrymen and cavalry, as well as 200 ships (these numbers are, of course, greatly disputed) he started the third Persian campaign against Greece. Just before the close of 481 B.C., the 32 Greek city-states held a Pan-Hellenic conference at Isthmus where it was decided:

- To stop their internecine wars and offer common resistance
- To allow all political exiles to return
- To punish those city-states that submitted to Persian authority. The King of Sparta, Leonidas, was appointed commander-in-chief of Greek land forces, while Admiral Euryviades, also of Sparta, was appointed commander-in-chief of the naval forces.

During his long march towards Greece, Xerxes passed through Asia Minor to Thrace, encountering no resistance. After that, Alexander, King of Macedonia, was compelled to follow Xerxes. Thessalia had already rendered homage to him and the Persian fleet was sailing parallel to the army. The Greeks, after dismissing the idea of offering resistance at the Tempi Pass, instead decided to array their army at Thermopylae and their naval forces at Artemisium. Thermopylae, a

From this point of view, one can see the number of hoplites on the vignette. Pieces of armour are strewn everywhere. It should also be noted the vegetation made from dried plants, natural roots, static grass and photo-etched ferns.

strategic choke point between Mount Oeta and the Malian Gulf was, at that time, quite a narrow passage through which only a cart could pass. The Persians were thus obliged to force that passage on their way to southern Greece.

On the battlefield, facing the huge Persian army, which also contained 10,000 "Immortals" under the command of Hydarnes, the Greeks arrayed a "bronze wall" consisting of the shields of about 7,000 hoplites, among them 300 Spartans.

At first, nothing happened and, for four days, the adversaries just stood and looked at each other. After these days had passed, Xerxes sent a messenger to Leonidas twice ordering him to surrender his arms. The Spartan king's answer was, "Come and get them!" and so, Xerxes, livid with anger, immediately ordered an attack. At the same time, Leonidas was offering sacrifice to Artemis and so the blood of the goat was the first to be spilt at the Battle of Thermopylae. More blood would be spilt over the following days, but everyone present was well aware of that.

The Persians, forming a body of 1,000 men (front) by 10, began marching towards the narrow passage, but the continuous narrowing of the path threw their formations into total disarray. The Persians began their first fruitless assault by their usual method – the Medean archers. At last, the mass of the Persian army crashed against the wall of the Greeks' shields – mainly Thespians' and Arcadians'. They formed a body 96 hoplites wide, dictated by the site's physical features. While the Persians were shouting "Xerxes wins!" the Greeks were answering with "Zeus Saviour!" Consecutive waves of attacking Persians were decimated by the Greek hoplites. Whenever possible, the Spartan phalanx, marching with total synchronization to the sound of the flute, advanced, unbeatable. By the end of the first day, a dozen Persian attacks had failed, and Xerxes is said to have leapt up off his seat from where he was watching the battle three times, trembling with fear for his army. The second day of the battle passed exactly as the first one, although Xerxes decided to eliminate his enemies by sending into the battle his elite corps, the "Immortals." Leonidas arrayed his Spartans in the front line and so, the "Immortals" failed to break the Spartan phalanx and had to retreat with heavy

Rear view of the vignette, where the third level of the base's groundwork can be seen one. Details of the hoplites' hair are also visible. Each of the locks of hair was made from a mixture of Magic Sculp and Duro epoxy putty, always with the thought of maintaining the correct scale.

The hoplite on the right bears two wounds, one on the thigh and another in the chest. Above him, his comrade is about to throw his broken spear at the enemy. The wounded officer with the bandaged thigh is ready to launch his last attack. Look closely at the ground's incline. This small vignette exhibits three different ground levels, necessary for the positioning of the seven figures in the restricted space of the base.

losses. On the third day, the Persians continued their attacks, but by midday, ten of these had failed. Then, the dark figure of Ephialtes from Anticyra of Malis appeared. He volunteered to guide the "Immortals," under the command of Orontes and Hydarnes, to the rear of the Greek forces for a handful of gold coins. The Persians were able, with Ephialtes as guide, to follow a narrow path along the ridge of Mt. Anopaea, called Anopaea Pass, later called "The Path of the "Immortals," and, after crossing the Asopus River they saw the Phocians guarding the passage before them. After firing a rain of arrows, they drove them away and finally reached a hill behind the mass of the Greek army. The beginning of the end of one of the most unequal battles in history had arrived. The Greek hoplites had reached the limits of the endurance and were, by now, exhausted.

Those who had survived up to that point were under no illusions about what was about to happen. Several Greek generals suggested they should withdraw and return home and continue their resistance from there. Leonidas accepted their request, but said that he and the remaining Spartans would remain behind as a rearguard to hold up the Persians for as long as possible. This rear-guard action would hold out for one more day, with a glorious death as a reward, to give the rest of the Greek army the opportunity to safely retreat. 700 Thespians under the command of Demophilus also voluntarily remained to assist the Spartans, although 400 Thebans were forced to do so. What is unknown, and more important unremembered by the majority, is that 900 Laconian Helots also fought in that last stand. The remainder of the allies (Corinthians, Locrians, Fleiasians, Mycenaeans and Arcadians) left the battlefield under cover of night. At dawn, the battle

The one and only Thespian on the vignette receives a deadly blow on his chest. The Spartan on the left belongs to the Geronthroi clan, as can be seen by the scorpion design on his shield, and holds a broken sword. The last of the hoplites are said to have fought with bare hands after their weapons were destroyed.

began again, but this time it was quite short, as most of the Greek hoplites, including Leonidas, fell almost immediately. The few who survived the first attack then withdrew to a small hill, called Colonus. There, at about 10 a.m., surrounded, they fell to the last man under a rain of arrows. Xerxes, as ordered, at last had Leonidas' head impaled on a spear.

The Battle of Thermopylae was fought at a strategically convenient site that held many advantages for the defenders to repulse the enemy but, unfortunately, its fate was decided by the treacherous role played by Ephialtes. However, it proved beyond doubt that a few Greeks could drive back the huge Persian army. It is also said that, if Leonidas had another 5,000 hoplites at his disposal, the outcome of the battle would have been very different.

This battle has left us with many events to be remembered. Here are the words of the Spartan king to his comrades during their last supper, "Let's now eat plainly, so that the food does not impede our movement. Tonight, we shall amply dine in the Kingdom of Pluto."

Herodotus wrote that when Dienekes, a Spartan warrior, was informed that Persian arrows would be so numerous as "to blot out the sun," he remarked, with characteristically laconic prose, "So much the better, we shall fight in the shade!"

Finally, below is Simonides' famous epigram, a symbol of obedience to country and laws: "Go tell the Spartans, passerby, that here, by Spartan law, we lie."

CONSTRUCTION

My intention was to represent the scene of the last moments of the Spartans on the Colonus hill, where they all fell to the last man under a rain of arrows. So, one of the first tasks was to make about 30 arrows. The wooden shafts were made of pins cut to length, while the feathers were made of thin plastic card; I also used the arrows supplied with the Andrea kit. The next step concerned the construction of the base, using as a basis the resin part by Andrea. Of course, during the construction process it actually became much bigger with the addition of epoxy putty, so that it could accommodate the seven figures of the vignette I had in mind. The positioning of the figures and the setting itself were altered many times during the construction process. From the start, I had decided

This view shows the way the incoming arrows are represented. Each one was carefully glued to the edge of the figures' weapons. In order to make the Thespian absolutely stable, I drilled a hole in his right leg up to the knee and inserted a metal pin.

the position of only four of the hoplites: the two dead ones, the hoplite holding the shield with the scorpion emblem and the officer in the foreground.

To construct the hoplite lying the face down on the ground, I used the figure of the dead early Roman from the Verlinden vignette No:1798, Victorious Celt (now discontinued). The major problem I faced was that the hoplite is integral with the base. So, I had to carefully remove him from the ground so as not to destroy the figure. After this was done, using a motor tool and a blade, I removed the bronze thigh protectors and the linen straps below his breastplate. I then replaced the head with another by Preiser on which a helmet from the Andrea kit was fitted. After that, I prepared the rest of the conversion. For most of this, I used a mixture of Magic Sculp and Duro epoxy putty in a 50:50 ratio while, for the hair, beard and horsehair crest I used pure Duro. I did the same for all the other conversions that I shall mention later. So, to begin with, all the detail that had been lost from the tunic and thighs had to be re-sculpted. Next, I had to reconstruct the lower part of the breastplate and re-sculpted the hair, beard and crest. On the helmet that I was using from the Andrea, the hair had to be sculpted while and the tail of the crest had to be lengthened.

After completing the conversions on the first hoplite, I continued with the building of the figure of the dead hoplite lying flat on the ground. I used Leonidas' head, arms and legs from the Andrea kit and the breastplate of the hoplite holding Leonidas from the same kit, while the tunic was re-sculpted. Next, the arms and legs were glued in the desired positions; building the second hoplite was completed with the sculpting of the hair and beard.

I then moved on to the next hoplite, that is, the one holding the shield with the scorpion emblem. I used, as a basis, Pegaso's 5th century hoplite (kit No: 54-180), but replaced the head and left arm

I used over 30 arrows that I had made myself, as well as the arrows from the Andrea kit, for this vignette. The Andrea arrows, already with pointed heads, were placed "in the air" to accentuate the drama of the whole scene. This is another view of the vignette, taken from a little higher position than that of any observer.

The nameplate on the base was scratch-built. The famous Simonides' epigram was scribed on the epoxy putty in ancient Greek script. After the signboard was painted and weathered, to give the appearance of an old piece of marble, it was fixed to the wooden base by four small pins.

holding the shield with others from the Andrea kit. In order to place some more emphasis on the drama of the scene, I broke the sword held in the right hand, while the hand holding the shield was glued in another, more appropriate position. Then, once again, I had to re-sculpt the tunic along the join of the arm with the body, as well as the hair. I then drilled a small hole in the hoplite's right leg and positioned an arrow in it.

It was now the turn of the Spartan officer's figure, which proved to be the most difficult of all. I used the arms, legs and body from an Andrea figure. However, this particular figure was wearing a linen breastplate, whereas I wanted a muscular cuirass. So, the original breastplate was removed and a new muscular cuirass, along with a new tunic, was sculpted, as the old ones had been destroyed while removing the linen breastplate. The figure's head with the Corinthian style helmet came from the spares box, while the crest is from the Andrea kit and is placed in such a way so that it represents a Spartan officer. Then, I sculpted the hair on the head and the horsehair on the crest and, finally, the bandage on the figure's right thigh.

While constructing the first four figures, I was thinking of how many more figures I could add to the vignette, as well as their poses. Finally, considering the limited space on the small base, I

This view clearly shows the cuts on the arm of the figure in the foreground. They were simulated with red Citadel ink and Humbrol gloss varnish. Look at the rain of arrows and the Spartan officer's rear. This particular figure needed more time for its construction than the others, as most of its parts had to be re-sculpted.

A close-up of the fallen hoplite. The design on his shield is the leopard, the emblem of the Pylos clan. Note the broken spear and the dropped greave beneath the officer's feet.

This view shows details of the two dead hoplites. The emblem on the first one's shield is the most common one on Spartan shields: the female demon Gorgo. However, it should be noted that this was also the name of Leonidas' wife. While he was preparing to march to Thermopylae, she asked her husband, the king, what she could do to prove equal of him. Leonidas replied, "Marry a good man and have good children."

decided that three more would suffice. In order to maintain the balance between the figures still standing and those that had been killed, one of them would be placed down on the ground, another positioned in the vignette's centre but higher than the others, with the final one down on his knees, as I didn't have this pose among the figures I had already built. So, I proceeded with their construction, first planning and test fitting the parts from several different figures.

The next hoplite would be fallen and to the left of the officer. Once again, I used the Pegaso hoplite figure as a basis. The right arm, holding an arrow embedded in his chest is from the Wounded Macedonian figure by EVD (kit No: CG 117), the left hand to the wrist is from the Andrea kit, while the hand is from Preiser and, finally, the head is again from Andrea. After I had changed the position of the arms and head, I sculpted the hair, the crest and the tunic sleeves.

A close-up view of the Thespian on the vignette. Clearly seen is the crescent of Melaina Aphrodite, a common design on Thespian shields, and the leather cap, which the hoplites wore under their helmet to protect their heads from the friction with the helmet's iron skull.

Two close-up views of the Spartan officer. The emblem on his shield is the "gorgoneion" of the Chalkioikos Athena (temple on the Spartan acropolis). Probably, while launching his last attack, he uttered the ancient Greek battle cry "Eleleu!"

I then moved on to the kneeling hoplite. This one is from the Ampuries Hoplite figure by EVD (kit no: CG 03). At first, I had to convert a standing hoplite to a kneeling one. This modification required the re-sculpting of a part of the tunic near the legs. The right arm is from Andrea, while the complete left one is from Preiser, as this particular hoplite is not holding a shield. In his right arm he holds a broken spear, with the point extended. The final job on this hoplite was to sculpt the hair and crest.

Constructing the figures was completed with the hoplite in the centre of the vignette. Because of his position, I wanted to make him as impressive as possible. I decided to present him as a Thespian at the moment of being struck with an arrow in the middle of the chest.

The body, legs, left arm and helmet are from Andrea. The right arm holding the sword, meanwhile, is from the Pegaso hoplite figure, while the head is from the Wounded Macedonian figure by EVD after, of course, I had removed the helmet. In addition, I repositioned the right knee and re-sculpted his hair and beard, as well as part of the tunic next to the sleeves.

With the assembly of this final figure, the initial, most difficult part of the whole construction process was at an end. It should be noted, however, that I used pins in every joint to secure their stability. I also used metal pins in the figures' feet for the same reason. After all the figures were ready, I made the final decisions concerning their positions on the base and drilled the holes to receive them.

PAINTING
Shields

Painting the hoplites' shields was quite a demanding job. As far as the designs on the faces are concerned, they have to be in sympathy with the historical period in which the battle took place as well as with the individual hoplite's city. In this particular case, using the famous and attractive "Λ" sign must be avoided at all costs as it was not adopted by the Spartans until after 424 B.C. For the hoplites I used the following emblems:
- The scorpion, emblem of the Geronthroi clan
- The leopard, emblem of the Pylos clan
- The gorgoneion of Chalkioikos Athena on the officer's shield
- Gorgo, the female demon who petrified its enemies with a simple gaze. This was a common pattern on Spartan shields, as it symbolised the

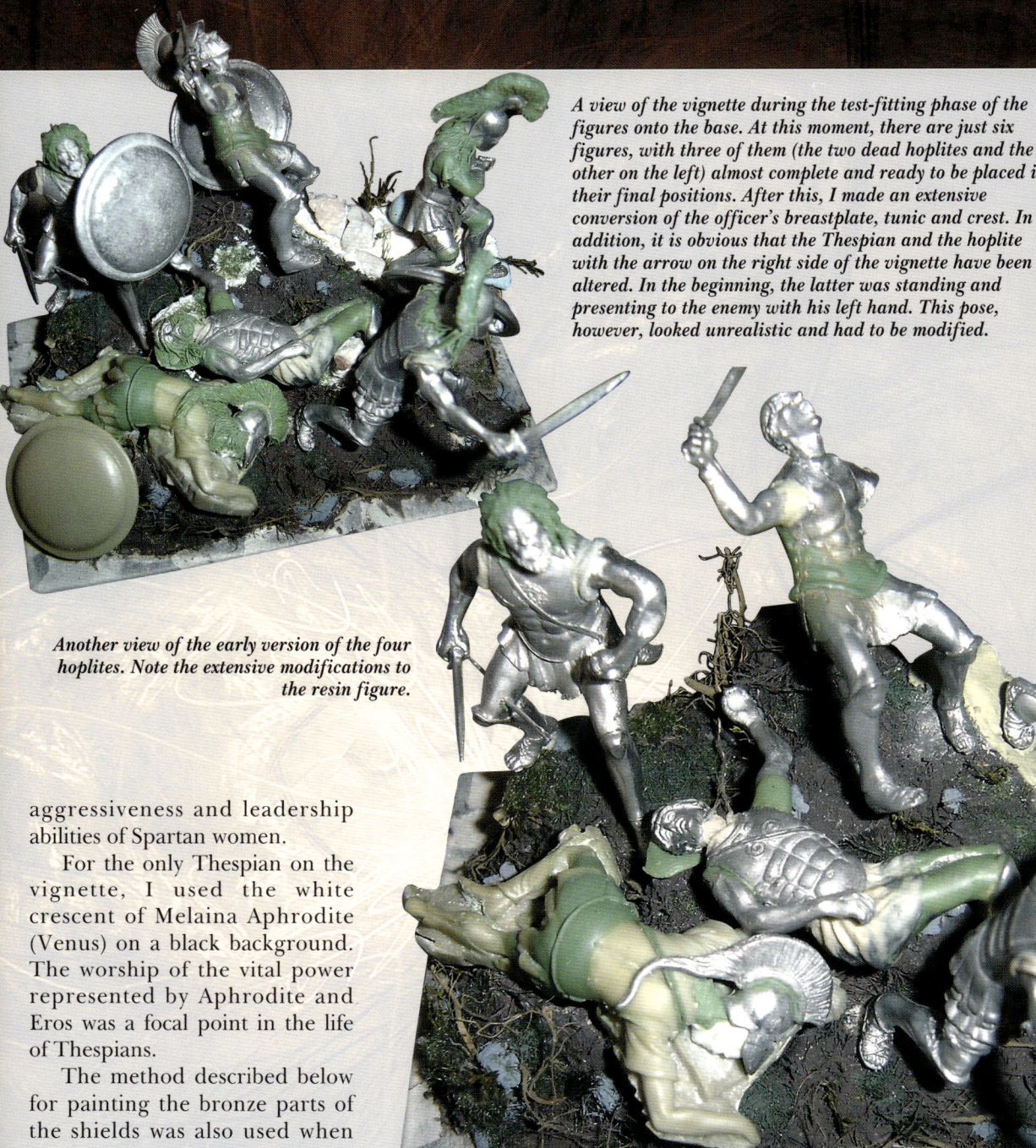

A view of the vignette during the test-fitting phase of the figures onto the base. At this moment, there are just six figures, with three of them (the two dead hoplites and the other on the left) almost complete and ready to be placed in their final positions. After this, I made an extensive conversion of the officer's breastplate, tunic and crest. In addition, it is obvious that the Thespian and the hoplite with the arrow on the right side of the vignette have been altered. In the beginning, the latter was standing and presenting to the enemy with his left hand. This pose, however, looked unrealistic and had to be modified.

Another view of the early version of the four hoplites. Note the extensive modifications to the resin figure.

aggressiveness and leadership abilities of Spartan women.

For the only Thespian on the vignette, I used the white crescent of Melaina Aphrodite (Venus) on a black background. The worship of the vital power represented by Aphrodite and Eros was a focal point in the life of Thespians.

The method described below for painting the bronze parts of the shields was also used when painting the helmets, breastplates and gaiters.

Before the painting process began, I tested the designs on the figures in order to define those areas that would be highlighted and shadowed, using of a lamp positioned above. The shields were all primed with Andrea AC-12. I began the painting process by painting the reverse of all the shields red.

Red Parts

Base: Venetian red (Winsor & Newton)
Highlights: base + Naples yellow (Winsor & Newton)
Shadows: base + mars black

Bronze Parts

I began the painting by applying a base coat of gold printers' ink. After allowing it dry for 24 hours, I applied a wash of a shade of raw umber - green. I left the shields to dry completely and then painted the shadows using a mixture of gold ink and burnt umber, taking advantage of the slower drying time to correct any mistakes by diluting the mixture when necessary. In those areas where there would be intense shadows, I added a little Winsor & Newton mars black oil paint to the mixture while still wet so that all the colours were completely

The figure of the early Roman from the Verlinden vignette is gradually being converted into a Spartan. Special care was needed while removing the figure from its base, into which it was integrated. Some plants can also be seen already attached to the base.

mixed. The highlights were done with gold ink, whereas I added a little silver printers' ink to the fresh gold one, only where necessary, for the final highlights. After all the colours had fully dried, the shields were given a very subtle wash of Winsor & Newton sap green oil paint to give them slightly oxidised appearance.

Black Shield

Base: mars black (Winsor & Newton)
Highlights: base + Payne's grey, mixed with the still wet base mixture, so that the colours were mixed properly.

The next step was to paint the emblems on the shields. They were painted with acrylic colours, taking great care to reproduce the correct highlights and shadows where necessary. Several bloodstains were represented using red Citadel ink, highlighting some of them with Humbrol gloss varnish. Finally, some sword/spear cuts were simulated with a fine brush. It was now time to proceed to the remaining parts of the hoplites. Once again, before starting to painting, everything was primed with Andrea AC-06 matt white.

Red Tunics and Crests

Base: basic red AC-12 + Napoleonic red
Highlights: base + ochre AC-15
Shadows: base + dark red AC-13

Where necessary, intense shadows were done using a wash of highly diluted matt black AC-26.

Skin Tone

Base: Yellow brilliant + burnt umber (by Winsor & Newton)
Highlights: base + titanium white
Shadows: base + burnt umber

Several scratches and wounds were simulated with a fine brush and red Citadel ink and then highlighted with gloss varnish.

Wooden Parts

To paint the wooden parts, I used Andrea AC-41 wood and then applied a wash of Winsor & Newton burnt umber oil paint.

The Geronthroi clan hoplite before the sword in his right hand was broken. As can be seen, this figure, as far as the conversion was concerned, was the easiest to build.

A Geronthroi clan hoplite, wounded by an arrow in his right thigh. Two more are embedded in his shield, while several more are stuck in the ground. The number of arrows in, and on the vignette was there to suggest that the Persian arrows could really "blot out the sun."

Metal Parts

For the metal parts, I used Vallejo Natural steel 864 and then gave them a wash with Winsor & Newton blue black.

Leather Parts

All the leather parts were painted with Andrea brown leather AC-42 and then given a wash with Winsor & Newton burnt umber. Any highlights were done with AC-12.

The identical colours that the black shield was painted with were also used for painting the Thespian's black linen breastplate and the black helmet crests. The white parts – the bandage, the white areas of the crests and the arrow feathers – were painted with Andrea matt white, AC-06, and shadowed with the addition of a little AC-26 matt black to the base mixture.

Hair and Beards

A mixture of matt black AC-26 + wood AC-41 was used for painting the black hair, with the highlights being done after adding a little matt white AC-06 to the base mixture and dry brushing it. The shadows, on the other hand, were represented with a wash of AC-26.

Dark brown AC-17 was used as the base colour for the brown hair. Highlights were done by dry brushing after adding a little wood AC-41 to the base colour; this time shadows were reproduced with a wash of AC-26.

GROUNDWORK

Constructing this vignette came to its conclusion with the making of the groundwork. I first prepared a mixture of Vallejo acrylic paste and AC-17 dark brown to construct the ground. I then applied this mixture over the whole surface of the base and, while it was still wet, I placed stones, static grass, roots, dried plants and weeds, as well as photo-etched ferns on some areas. The stones were painted with AC-17, while the grass and the plants were given a coat of olive green AC-03 and then highlighted by dry brushing after adding basic

This hoplite is very likely to be killed very soon, judging by the arrow that is already embedded in his helmet. Note, in the middle of the chaos of battle, he carries no shield, which was equal to certain death on an ancient battlefield.

yellow AC-07 to the base colour. The whole of the ground surface was given a wash with brown and black oil paints. Dry brushing with confederate grey highlighted any details on the stones, whereas the remainder of the groundwork was dry brushed with English khaki.

After four months of hard work, t was at last time to complete this vignette by positioning the hoplites on the base. Before placing them in their final position, I carefully drilled some tiny holes into the shields and the hoplites' bodies so that I could glue the arrows in them. Then, the figures were glued into position and all the remaining arrows were stuck into the ground. Some scattered objects, including broken swords, spears, a helmet and a greave, intensified the drama and tension of the scene.

Finally, I attached those arrows that were to be given the impression that they were still in the air. To achieve this, I had held back the Andrea arrows as they had sharp points. These were carefully randomly glued onto the edges of various weapons and other arrows, adding yet more realism and excitement to the small vignette.

BASE INSCRIPTION

I created a nameplate, suitable for this particular vignette, from Plasticard, cut to the correct size. I then covered its surface with a mixture of Magic Sculp and Duro epoxy putty. After consulting a book on ancient Greek script, I engraved the Simonides' famous epigram, "Go tell the Spartans, passerby, that here, by Spartan law, we lie." When the putty had completely dried, the inscription was painted on it in acrylic white, while the relief detail was highlighted and given a wash of burnt umber oil paint. Finally, the nameplate was glued to the wooden base.

CONCLUSION

The Battle of Thermopylae, which was fought at the height of the summer of 480 B.C., is one of the major cornerstones of Greek History. As far as modelling is concerned, it is a very popular theme worldwide, either as a vignette such as this, or just the figure of Leonidas. With a little patience and imagination, a small part of this glorious battle can decorate your showcase through model making, which is the three-dimensional representation of history itself.

Spartan Officer
Battle of Thermopylae

Thermopylae, 480 B.C. A few, but very brave men, made a last stand against the hordes of the Persian king, Xerxes, showing the way for the rest of the Greeks to resist. The self-sacrifice of these warriors inspired the people of the time, and continues to do so even for the Greek citizen of today.

CHRISTOS PANAYOTOPOULOS

150 mm
Spartan Officer: Athens Miniatures (AM-03)
Acrylic colors: Vallejo

Athens Miniatures is a company that has only recently enthusiastically entered the world of miniatures, bringing with it some pleasant surprises with every new release. The subject of this article, the bust of a Spartan officer from the Battle of Thermopylae, is one such surprise.

The kit consists of just three pieces of white metal, a helmet, its distinctive Spartan crest, and the bust's main body. The casting is absolutely amazing, as it should be as it has been done by the master caster, Ray Lamb of Poste Militaire. A quick cleaning off of the flash was sufficient, before pinning the bust to a base and priming it.

PAINTING THE FACE

When painting any bust, the most important area is the face. So, as only this will reveal the figure's character, it is imperative that you take great care when painting it and put in your best work. I decided to give the face the sunburned appearance of a man and warrior who has spent a lot of time in the sun. Also, even today, the Spartans are, generally speaking, sun tanned people.

For the flesh base coat I used a mixture of the following acrylic colors: matt flesh, red, black, english Uniform, beige brown and a little violet. I added a little more Black to the mixture to obtain the dark tone I wanted, and then painted the face with the base coat. For the shadows, I added the following to the base mixture, some black, English uniform, beige brown red and violet. I applied six coats of shadowing to complete this process. I then moved on to the highlights, adding some matt flesh and a little magenta to the base mixture. After giving it several coats, I stopped adding matt flesh, but kept on adding light flesh and a bit of magenta. For the final 2-3 highlights, I included a little off-white to the mixture.

When the highlighting was complete, I began with some washes to add some more "life" to the face. With highly diluted red, I passed it below the nose, the cheeks, the nostrils and the temples on the sides of the head. Next, with highly diluted turquoise, I toned in the "eye bags." Then, mixing it with English uniform, also highly diluted, I made a pass under the chin, the lower lip, behind the ears, and around the edges of the beard.

With all these

The tonal variations impart a realistic look and all the bust's elements come together very harmoniously. The shadowing and highlighting on the face requires lots of patience, as there are large areas to cover.

washes, adding different tones, I ensured that the face was much more interesting and alive. To paint the lips, I added some red to the base mixture and gave them a number of light coats to achieve a reddish tone.

The hair and beard were painted with a mixture of black, green ochre, and a little violet. I then used solid black for the shadows while, for the highlights, I lightened the base mixture with green ochre and English uniform. Where I desired a gray tone, I added some off-white to the base mixture.

METAL PARTS (CHEST – HELMET)

To paint the breastplate and the helmet, I decided against using acrylics, using printers' inks instead, to show off these large surfaces to better effect.

As a base mixture for the breastplate, I used the Gold from Oakwood Studios, with some Old Gold from the same company's range (adding a reddish tone) and some burnt umber oil paint. The mixture was carefully painted onto the surfaces. I then "baked" the bust in the oven to speed up the paint's drying time. Then, I added the shadows using burnt umber oil paint, taking care not to "lift" the underlying coat. After each shadow tone, I baked the bust, returning it to the oven. I used the same procedure for the highlighting, after adding pure gold to the base mixture. To paint the helmet, I followed the same procedure, but the base mixture included some more Old Gold to give a different tone.

CLOTH

For the tunic, I decided on a red color, as the Spartans always wore red or black clothing in battle. As the cloak would also be in a shade of red, it had to be a harmonious combination. As a base mixture for the tunic, I used scarlet, red, black, and a little violet. For the shadows, I added Black to the base mixture, while for the highlights I first added some Scarlet to the base mixture and, then, for further highlights, I added more scarlet and matt flesh. The Spartan tunics were a very particular piece of clothing. Each young man received one when he reached maturity and if he succeeded in becoming an "equal." The color of it was a relatively dark red, made so with the intention of hiding the blood of a battle wound.

Painting the shadows and highlights, even on the rear of the figure, demand lots of attention, and are also very important.

Note the characteristics of the face. It is obviously a sun-tanned Spartan warrior.

For the cloak, I used a base coat of a mixture of red, black, deep orange, violet, turquoise, scarlet and burnt umber. Then, for shadows, I added, black, violet, and turquoise (take care with the quantities, especially of the turquoise!). Highlighting was done after adding more red, scarlet, deep orange and Violet to the base mixture. After a number of passes, I added some more deep orange until I was happy with the highlighting so far. To complete the highlighting process, I gave them a light wash of highly diluted base mixture.

For the crest, I made a base mixture of red, magenta, black and violet. I then shadowed with black and highlighted after adding more red, magenta, and violet to the base mixture. Once again, after completing the painting of the highlights, I gave them a light wash of the base mixture.

I completed the bust in the space of just four evenings and, I must admit, the whole operation gave me great pleasure. If you follow my example, I hope you gain as much pleasure while adding a fine Greek subject to your miniature collection.

Greek Hoplite

BABIS STATHIS

A beautifully sculpted figure will always attract a figure modeller's attention. This particular Greek hoplite, sculpted by Andriano Laruccia, is one such figure; it is considered to be one of the best, especially by those who love is assembling and painting subjects from ancient Greek history. So, as I wanted to participate in the Nations Trophy competition, I decided to assemble and paint it. After studying some well-documented historical reference, I knew what colors, painting patterns and designs I was going to use. The shield is most important and adds immensely to the overall quality of the figure and so special care must be taken when painting it. This particular design ("gorgonion") is from the Museum of Ancient Olympia and was, at the time, a very popular shield design among the hoplites.

54 mm
Greek Hoplite, Italy, 5th century: EMI Productions, Gladius GLC-11
Acrylic colors: Vallejo, Andrea
Oil paints: Winsor & Newton
Epoxy putty: Magic Sculp
Typographical ink: gold

Left-side view of the vignette. Note the hoplite's helmet, the shield pattern ("gorgonion") and the realistic groundwork (rocks, water, plants).

PAINTING

Face
Base: flat flesh 955 + blue violet 811 + vermillion red 909 + magenta 945 + English uniform (Andrea color)
Highlights: base + sunny skin tone 845
Final highlights: + base skin tone 815
Shadows: base + khaki + vermillion 909
Final shadows: + flat brown 984

Linen Breastplate
Base: sky grey 989 + beige 821 + pale sand
Highlights: base + pale sand + off white 70820
Shadows: base + beige 821 + sky grey 989

Upper Part of the Linen Breastplate - Shield
Base: Oxford blue 807 + black 950
Highlights: base + sky grey 989
Shadows: base + black 950

Shield Pattern
Base: pale blue 906 + sky grey 989
Highlights: base + off white 70820
Shadows: base + a touch of black 950

Tunic

Base: Andrea basic red + Prussian blue 965 + violet 812
Highlights: base + basic red
Final highlights: highlights + orange red 910 + sunny skin tone 845
Shadows: base + Prussian blue 965
Final shadows: shadows + black 950

Cape

Base: blue violet 811 + sunny skin tone 845
Highlights: base + sunny skin tone 845
Shadows: base + black 950

I also added a little burnt umber 941 to the shadow mixture in order to paint some areas of the cape that I wanted to look dirtier.

Metal Parts

Base: acrylic gold + copper + burnt umber 941 + orange brown 981
Highlights: gold ink
Shadows: burnt umber + black oil paints

BASE

The rocks were created from Magic Sculp epoxy putty; they were then painted with grey – earthy tones. The water was made from Pattex epoxy glue using three thin coats with the addition of a touch of burnt umber oil paint. Before spreading the water, the riverbed was painted with burnt umber 941 and black green 980. I also attached several small dry roots onto the base, along with some small bushes and weeds, positioning them among the rocks to integrate them properly with the overall setting.

A close-up of the hoplite's shield. The "gorgonion" (the designs featured either the head of Medusa, (to frighten the hoplites' opponents to death!), or the head of the mermaid Gorgo, used to protect the shield-bearer. Both were, according to knowledgable authorities, quite common designs on the shields of 5th century Greek hoplites.

Head-on view of the Greek hoplite figure. One can see the detail on the linen breastplate as well as in the inside of the shield and the groundwork.

Rear view of the hoplite. The excellent detail on the rear of the shield, the realistic designs on the cloak, as well as the small plants attached to the base, immediately draw the viewers eye.

Greek "Siceliota"

CHRISTOS KATSELOS

A wonderful release by this Italian company was this beautiful figure of a Greek hoplite in Sicily.

> **54 mm**
> Greek "Siceliota" Hoplite, 5th century B.C. with Thracian Helmet: Romeo Models (RM 54-055)
>
> Acrylic colors: Vallejo
> Oil Paints: Winsor and Newton
> Other colors: Printers' Inks
> Enamel colors: Humbrol
> Primer: Citadel – White Skull
> Putty: Magic Sculp, Vallejo
> Pigments: Mig Productions

The quality of the casting is beyond reproach, and the cleaning and preparation required was minimal. The figure was then given a thorough wash, using a brush and washing-up liquid. Where required, a fine file or sandpaper was used. Some parts of the figure – especially the shield – were then polished with the use of a Dremel motor tool and a soft wire brush.

I drilled some holes in the joints as I felt they needed strengthening. Special care must be taken with the left hand as it carries the shield and needs some extra reinforcement. Any gaps were filled with Magic Sculp epoxy putty. The figure was fixed to a temporary block and then primed with Citadel spray primer.

PAINTING

The figure was painted with Vallejo acrylic colors, except for the metal parts where I used oil colors and printers' inks.

Flesh

The flesh was painted with a base mixture of brown sand + basic skin tone + red leather + burnt cadmium red in the relative proportions of 4:1:1:0,5. For highlights, I gradually added basic skin tone to the base mixture (making 4-5 different shades) while, for the final highlights, I used base + basic skin tone + light flesh. For the shadowing, I used base + burnt cadmium red while, for the deeper ones, I added black/red.

Below is a table showing the proportions of diluting the colours:

	Parts of color	Parts of distilled water
Base	1	1
Highlights/Shadows	1	4-5
Details	1	2
Outlining	1	10
Mid-tones – Blending mixes	1	20

Red

The red areas of the clothing and crest were painted with a mixture of vermillion + red + brown beige + black red. To avoid monotony, I simply altered the quantity of vermillion to get a slightly different tone.

For the highlights, I gradually added vermillion + light orange and, finally, a little sunny skin tone.

For the shadows, I gradually added burnt cadmium red, with a little black red at the end.

Where some outlining was needed, I used a highly diluted mixture of black red + black (as indicated in the previous table)

In order to blend in any strong contrasts on the transition areas between light and shadows, I used soft glazes of highly diluted red (diluted in a proportion 1:20). The number of passes should be in proportion to the

Head on view of the hoplite figure.

The pose of the completed figure is very realistic.

SHIELD

Painting the shield was comparatively easy, although a bit complicated and needs a little time to make a good job of it.

It was first given a coat of an acrylic mixture of black + Prussian blue + burnt umber. When this was dry, it was given a second coat of more Humbrol clear black, resulting in a slightly gloss surface. After around 5-10 minutes, with the help of an old brush, and white spirit (or turpentine, if you prefer something stronger), parts of the second coat were removed, until the right degree of weathering was reached.

A hobby knife can be used for more intense weathering and for simulating any possible damage.

The scorpion design was sketched on paper and then transferred onto the shield's surface. The color of the scorpion is an acrylic mixture of red beige + red leather + yellow ochre. A number of areas were highlighted with red beige + yellow ochre, while others were shaded with red leather + a little vermillion. The shield's surface was given a number of "cuts" that were painted in shades of gray and black and even gold in the deeper cuts.

strength of the contrast that needs to be blended in.

For the gold-colored metal parts, use acrylics, oil paints and printers' inks.

Gold Parts

Base (acrylic mixture): gold + old gold + burnt umber + gloss black + English Uniform
Base (oil - inks mixture): gold (ink) + burnt umber (W&N oil) + black (W&N oil)
Highlights: base + gold (ink)
Shadows: base + burnt umber + black (to finish)

Sword

Base (acrylic): gloss black + burnt umber
Base (oil – inks): silver (ink) + black (W&N oil) + burnt umber (W&N oil)
Highlights: Base + silver (ink)
Shadows: Base + burnt umber and finally black (W&N oil)

For weathering, use different tones of brown and black.

Several cuts on the surface of the shield add realism to the completed figure. Where the colour has not been weathered, it has a satin finish, otherwise it is matt and toned down.

BASE

The base was relatively simple. The ground was formed using Magic Sculp to which some pebbles were added and, finally, it was covered with a mixture of Vallejo acrylic putty + Mig Pigments + brown. Before this completely dried, some vegetation and static grass was added The vegetation was painted with several shades of green, the ground with brown tones, and Mig pigments were then used over the whole base.

Alexander the Great
King of the World

ALAIN DE BUSSE

90 mm
Alexander the Great: Pegaso (90-903)
Macedonian Guards Infantryman IV C. B.C.:
Pegaso (90-024), now discontinued.

Enamel colours: Humbrol
Oil paints: Winsor & Newton
Brushes: Winsor & Newton

Between the great civilian and military personalities of world history, there is one that stands out, as his achievements outshine those of anybody else. Of course, we must be referring to Alexander the Greek, who — rightly — history has labelled "the Great." In the next few pages, I shall present this legendary figure in 90 mm, using the respective Pegaso kit as a starting point.

Overall view of the vignette. The painting techniques described in the text, as well as the outstanding quality of the Italian company's figures result in an eye-catching scene, full of strength and action.

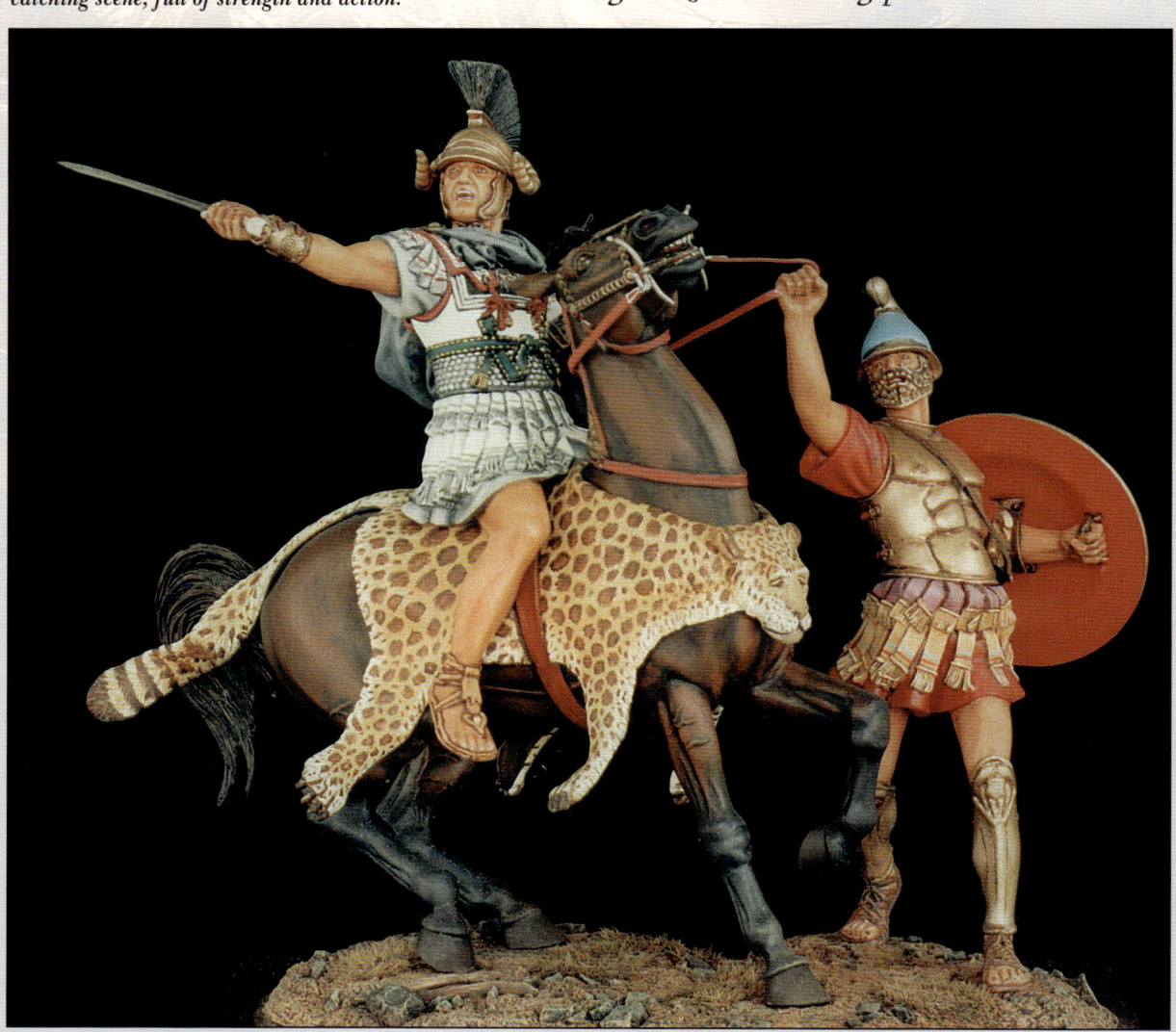

Since the history of the greatest military leader of all time is already well known and is, therefore, unnecessary to go through it again, I shall move straight on to describing the construction and painting of the figures. The vignette contains two separate Pegaso figures: one being the mounted Alexander and the other his servant.

Starting with the Alexander figure, I can say that the mould lines are both subtle and unobtrusive; the parts fit is excellent, requiring just the minimum filler. In most instances the joins requiring filler were hidden by other parts with the sole exception of the lion's head that required a little more filler. The rein by which the servant holds his master's horse was replaced with another much longer one. In total, the Alexander figure consists of 27 parts.

The servant's figure consists of 13 parts, one of which is supplied as an alternative part in the case of a modeller not wanting him to hold the horse's rein but his sword instead. The fit of this figure is also excellent, with absolutely no flash. I used filler just along the join between two separate bases to amalgamate them into a single base. As already mentioned in previous articles, before priming any figure, it must first be cleaned with wire wool or a copper brush so that any white metal imperfections are eliminated. After completing the burnishing of the servant figure, I glued the legs together and attached them to the body. After that, I drilled holes and inserted pins in the hands and head, before they too were glued into position. These pins are really necessary to prevent any parts breaking off at a later date because of their weight. After the figure was fixed to a temporary base, so that I could paint it more easily, I primed it with matt Humbrol 34 and left it to dry. I was now ready to continue with the most interesting part of the whole procedure, that of painting!

Humbrol flesh 61 was used as the base undercoat for the face, hands and legs. After which I went over these parts with the correct tones using burnt sienna and yellow ochre oil paints in a 50:50 ratio. Next (and after the flesh had dried completely), I applied a highly diluted coat of the oil paint mixture and, before it had dried, I highlighted selected areas with white oil paint. I then painted the shadows, using a mixture of mars brown and burnt sienna oil paints in the appropriate ratios, to accentuate the appropriate areas. After that, I moved on to some more intense highlighting using the earlier flesh mixture and adding white to it.

The two bases, that of Alexander and his servant, were butted together and any gap filled with putty.

Burnt umber was used for the eyelids, titanium white for the outlines, burnt umber for the pupils and black for the irises.

With the flesh tones complete, I turned to the tunic. For this, I chose Humbrol matt 153 as an undercoat, alizarin crimson for the base mixture and scarlet for the highlights.

For the straps holding the cuirass, I used yellow ochre and titanium white oil paints in a 3/10 ratio over the primer and then (after they had fully dried) I applied a wash of highly diluted burnt umber to accentuate the fringes. I then moved on to the highlights, using titanium white with the addition of very little yellow ochre to dull it down a bit. The remainder of the cloth was painted with purple and white. The lines were painted with blue and red enamel colours but after the oil paints had completed dried.

Rear view of the figures. The painting of the portrait on the shield as well as the lion's skin was a somewhat painstaking job, but the end result was well worth the effort.

The cuirass, the gaiters and the helmet were first given a coat of diluted burnt umber and then (after allowing it to dry completely) they were given a second coat of a mixture consisting of burnt umber and gold 16. For the highlights, I used gold (liquid leaf), with burnt umber was once again being used for the shadows. The cuirass straps were painted with mars brown over a basecoat of Humbrol matt 153.

The mask of the helmet was first painted with gold 16 and then it given a wash of burnt umber. Next, I dry-brushed it with gold, while for the helmet's blue colour I mixed matt 25 with French ultramarine and titanium white oil paints.

The sandals were painted with 63, followed by a wash of burnt umber oil paint. The sword scabbard was painted black and then given a wash of mars brown, while its gold mounts were painted with gold 16. The rear of the shield was painted red, using the same mixtures as for the tunic, while for the design on the front I chose one of the many recommended by Pegaso.

The same procedure was followed for the preparation of the Alexander figure, which is based on the famous mosaic in Pompeii. All the colors and representations are based on this particular mosaic. The only, and primary difference is that, in this instance, Alexander wears a helmet. So, the face, hands and legs were painted following the above-mentioned procedure. The belt was painted in the following way: after I had outlined it with black oil paint, I moved on to the reverse side and painted it with green oil paint over the primer. Before it had dried completely, I highlighted it with a little white, spreading it over the appropriate areas. I then, applied some small spots on the top and bottom of the inside of the belt using yellow enamel colour.

The Macedonian hoplite is supplied as a separate figure – apart from Alexander – and can be posed on his own, holding a sword in his right hand.

While the figure of Alexander was quite a quite demanding model, the complex painting techniques will fully compensate the modeller for his efforts.

The robe was painted with a mixture of black and white oil paints (producing grey!) in a ratio so that the result was darker than the tunic that was also grey. Next, on the still fresh grey oil paint, I applied white highlights and black shadows. After leaving it to dry, I applied more intense highlights using light grey oil paint.

The helmet and the wrist protectors were painted in the same way as the servant's, while the crest was painted black and then dry-brushed with grey. After gluing the horse together and priming it, it was given a base coat of Humbrol matt 63 and then a much thinner one of Van Dyck brown. I then removed the excess paint with a clean, completely dry brush so that only a thin coat of paint remained on the surface. This process accentuated the horse's anatomy and also showed me where to apply the highlights using burnt umber oil paint and the shadows with black. With that, I had reached, to my mind, the most interesting and attractive part of the whole painting process, that of the leopard skin that, when complete, would bring out the figure's details even more clearly. I had already painted the reverse with grey and brown tones before gluing it on the horse. I now moved on to priming the outer surface and giving it a coat of Humbrol matt 63. I next applied a mixture of yellow ochre and white in the same way as I had already done with the horse and, while it was still wet, I highlighted it with some white.

Using a photo of an actual leopard – after the skin's base tone had dried – I painted the outlines of the spots with thinned burnt umber. Before this had time to dry, I painted the interior of each spot with thinned mars brown, taking care to follow the direction of the fur, this being quite visible.

When this was completed and dried, it was time to mount Alexander on his horse. In addition to the metal pins, I also used two-part epoxy glue to make him an even more permanent fixture! I also used the same glue to fix the vignette base onto the larger, wooden one, and the two figures into their proper position. The final item that had to be glued was the horse's rein, after replacing it with another, made from thin aluminium foil.

So, all in all, to me, this is an almost perfect vignette from any angle. To my mind, it should surely be a part of your collection… sooner or later.

Mongol Warrior

BABIS STATHIS

60 mm
Scratch-built figure
Acrylic colours: Vallejo, Andrea
Oil paints: Winsor & Newton
Epoxy putty: A + B, Duro, Magic Sculp

Building a scratch-built figure is, without doubt, a very difficult undertaking as it requires some knowledge of anatomy, good observational skills, lots of imagination and a good deal of experience! I began the construction process by first making a 60 mm armature out of copper wire. Next, the skull, chest, pelvis and some basic muscular groups (i.e. biceps, quadriceps, etc.) were sculpted from A+B putty, leaving a small gap at the joints. Then, by bending these joints, I was able get the figure into the desired pose. After I had achieved the action pose I wanted, I could then proceed with the rest of the figure's anatomy. Giving the figure the right proportions and correct anatomy is most essential, especially at this juncture of its construction, as any mistake here will reflect in the completed figure and it will soon become very noticeable to anybody viewing the final result, no matter how well it has been painted. So, one should devote as much time as needed to measure the figure's overall dimensions again and again before moving to the next step.

FACE

The face is literally, the "heart" of the figure. Careful observation of photographs will impart to the figure modeller the correct distinctiveness of the facial characteristics of the figure they wish to sculpt. So, in this case, prominent cheekbones, Chinese-looking eyes, soft, large eyebrows and, finally, a short, oblate nose were sculpted on the surface of the face, to give the characteristic look of a Mongol's face. The next step was to "dress" the figure according to its motion and pose so that the folds of the clothing fall in the correct way. The medium mixture I used to sculpt the figure was 70% A+B and 30% Duro putty. This gave me ample time to shape it into the correct shapes, as this particular mixture dries slowly and is very workable.

PAINTING

Face

The numbers refer to Andrea Acrylics
Base: flat flesh 955 + blue violet 811 + ochre brown 856 + vermillion red 909 + magenta 945 + English uniform
Highlights: base + sunny skin tone 845
Final highlights: as with highlights + basic skin tone 815
Shadows: basic + khaki + vermillion red 909
Final highlights: as with shadows + flat brown 984

The pose of the completed figure is very realistic.

Tunic - Sleeves
Base: pale blue 906 + pastel grey 885 + basic skin tone 815
Highlights: base + basic skin tone 815
Final highlights: as with highlights + pale sand
Shadows: base + black 950

Leather Parts – Shield
Base: medium brown 826 + black 950 + bright orange 851
Highlights: base + a little bright orange
Shadows: base + a little black 950

Trousers
Base: sky grey 989 + beige 821 + pale sand
Highlights: base + pale sand + off-white 70820
Shadows: base + beige 821 + black 950

Leather Coat
Base: burnt umber 941 + flat yellow 953 + blue violet 811 + basic skin tone 815
Highlights: base + a little basic skin tone 815
Shadows: base + a little black 950

Boots
Base: brown sand 876 + sky grey 989 + beige red 804
Highlights: base + basic skin tone 815
Final highlights: as with Highlights + pale sand
Shadows: base + burnt umber 941

Metal Parts
Base: acrylic gold + copper + burnt umber 941 + orange brown 981
Highlights: gold ink
Shadows: burnt umber + black oil paints

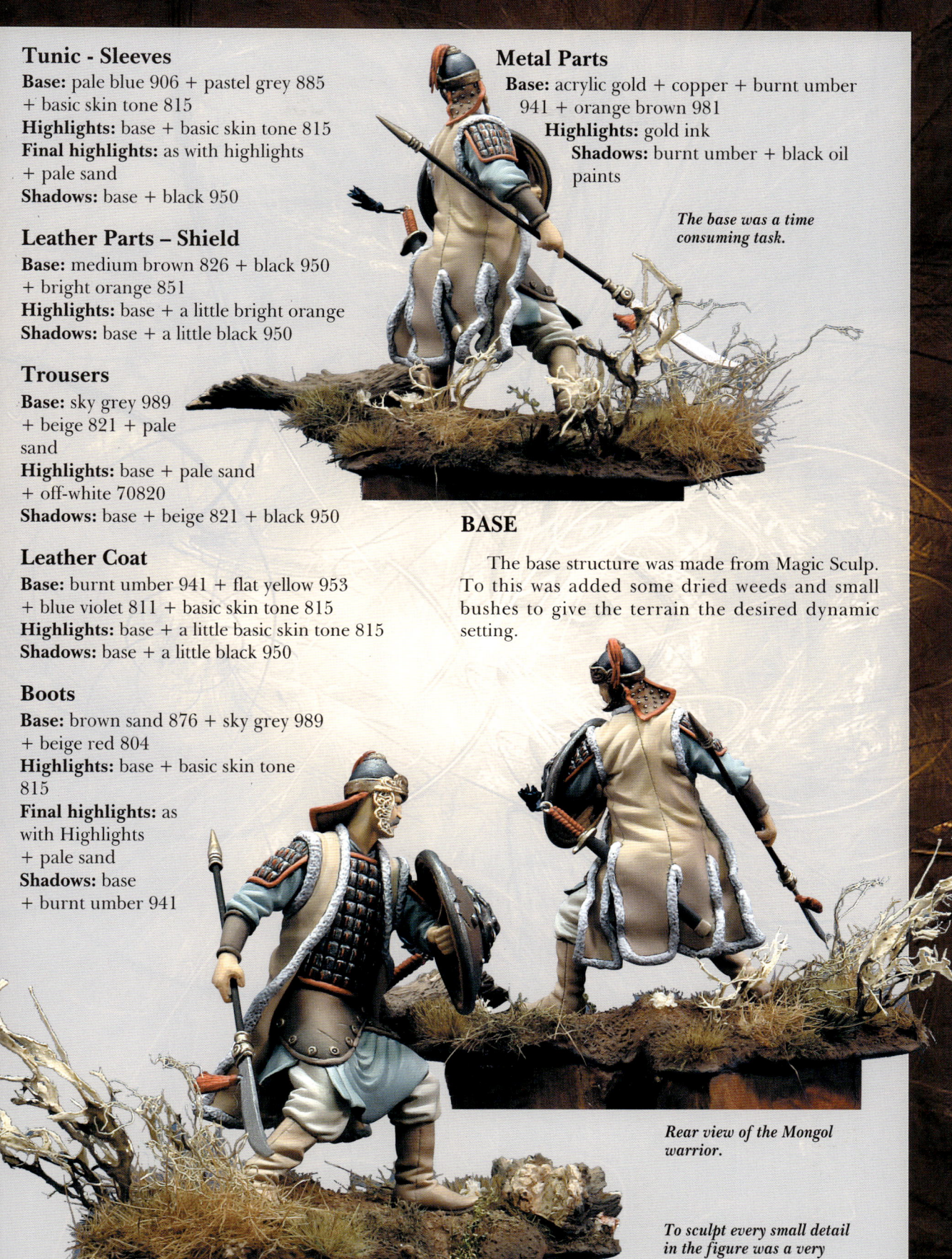

The base was a time consuming task.

BASE
The base structure was made from Magic Sculp. To this was added some dried weeds and small bushes to give the terrain the desired dynamic setting.

Rear view of the Mongol warrior.

To sculpt every small detail in the figure was a very difficult work.

Step by Step
PAINTING FACES WITH ACRYLIC COLORS

In this article, we will discover the secrets of the famous Maltese modeler Ray Farrugia. All color codes are from Vallejo paint range, but each modeler should use the make of acrylic paint he prefers, finding the correct color tone from the corresponding charts. (Editor's note)

90 mm
Mameluk: Poste Militaire -
Roman Legatus: Pegaso Models (90-007)
Acrylic Colors: Vallejo, Andrea (AC)

TEXT – PHOTOGRAPHS:
RAY FARRUGIA

After the casting flash has been cleaned off, including any possible mould lines or other blemishes from the surface of the two heads, they were primed ready to get on with the painting. I always begin with the eyes, so the figures soon gain some "character," after which I continue with painting the skin. The mixtures that were used for each of the two cases are indicated below.

MAMELUK
Base: 921 English khaki + 909 vermillion + 845 sunny skin tone + 850 medium olive
Highlights: base + 845 sunny skin tone
Final highlights: highlights + 955 matt flesh
Shadows: diluted 950 black + 909 vermillion
Beard area: diluted 950 black + AC-22 Prussian blue

To give the face a tired look, use a wash of AC-22 Prussian blue around the eye bags area.

Finally, I use washes of intense 851 orange or 909 vermillion, or a mixture of these two colors, on the back of the cheeks, above the eyes, the sides of the nose, the moustache area, and the sides of the chin's upper surface.

ROMAN OFFICER
Base: AC-02 English khaki + 909 vermillion + 845 sunny skin tone
Highlights: base + 845 sunny skin tone + 860 medium flesh
Final highlights: highlights + 955 matt flesh + 815 basic skin tone + 928 light flesh
Shadows: 950 black + 909 vermillion
Beard area: 950 black + diluted AC-22 Prussian blue

To give the face a tired look, I use a wash of AC-22 Prussian Blue around the eye bags area.

Finally, I use washes of intense orange 851 or 909 vermillion, or a mixture of these two colors, on the back of the cheeks, above the eyes, the sides of the nose, the moustache area, and the sides of the upper surface of the chin.

The final photos shows the completed painted faces after being given a coat of satin varnish. This gives the painted area a uniform look and makes the faces more realistic.

  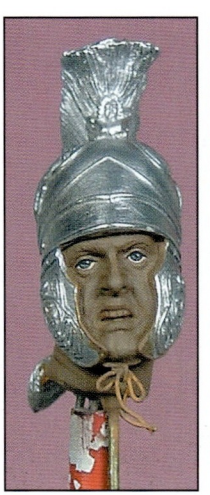   

The figure of the Roman Officer, from which I painted the head.

Step by Step

MAMELUK

This is definitely one of the finest figures produced by Poste Militaire. It was sculpted by one of the best sculptors around, Julian Hullis!! It's a 90 mm Mameluk.

TEXT – PHOTOGRAPHS: RAY FARRUGIA

90 mm
Mameluk: Poste Militaire
Acrylic colors: Maimeri, Vallejo, Andrea
Oil colors: Winsor & Newton

FACE

Base: raw sienna + orange yellow + yellow ochre + brilliant green deep (dab) + burnt sienna
Highlights: base + yellow ochre + yellow orange
Final highlights: highlights + yellow ochre + flesh tint + Naples yellow
Shadows: violet (diluted glaze)
Beard area: navy blue (diluted glaze)
Final shadows: black + primary red

Photos 23 - 33 show the painting of the helmet neck cloth, the border of the same cover and the helmet.

Photos 1 – 7 reveal the innate beauty of metal castings when they are done by the master and have become a benchmark for most figure kits' manufacturers! After the usual clean up of the parts was completed, the torso, legs and arms were glued together. I always insert pin into the parts before assembly as this makes a secure bond! I never tire of emphasizing the use of pins as, apart from ensuring a secure bond between the heavier parts, for the smaller sub-assemblies, it also adds a "holding point."

Photo 10 shows the bare terrain that was constructed from pieces of cork bark glued to the wooden base to form a rocky ledge from where he mameluk is scouting the lower terrain for any signs of the enemy. Dried shrubs and flowers were also added at this point.

As always, I begin by painting the face, as this gives me the impetus to drive forward! I use extra care while doing this as the face can make or break any figure. Photos 11 to 22 are the step-by-step process. Recently, I have begun using Maimeri tube acrylics and these are much like tube oils...that is to say, you have to really mix the paint to achieve a good mixture! The following is how I set about this face, which is an Arabic olive-skinned native. Unless specified otherwise, all colours are Maimeri.

NOTES:

V: Vallejo colors
A: Andrea colors

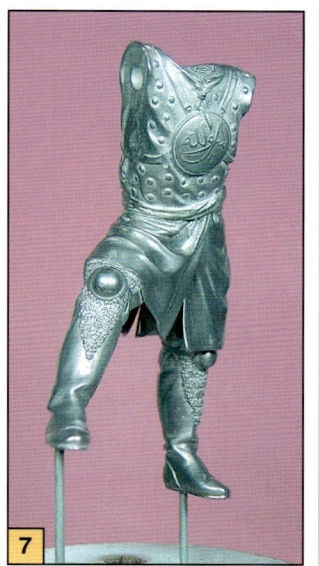
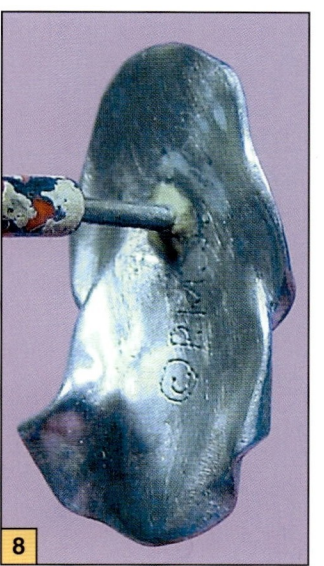
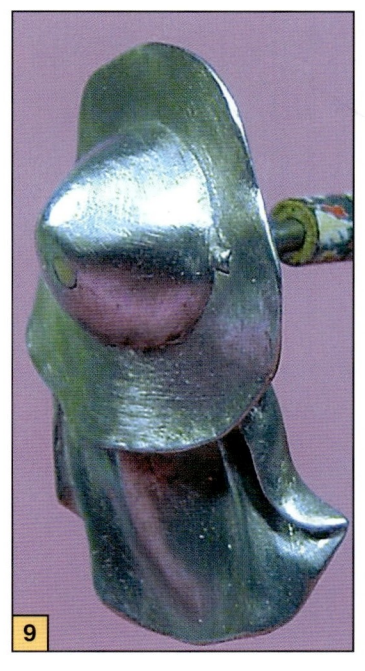

Step by Step

12

13

14

15

16

17

18

19

20

21

22

23

24

25

26

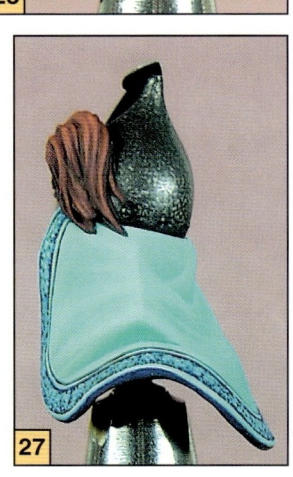
27

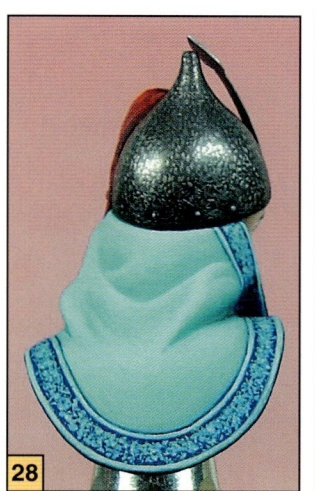

Step by Step

35

36

37

38

39

40

41

42

43

HELMET CLOTH COVER

Base: turquoise blue
Highlights: base + emerald green
Final highlights: highlights + white
Shadows: primary blue
Final shadows: highlights + black

The border of neck cloth was conjured up in my mind and, Yes, it's actually a MESS ...let me explain! During the latter stages of WWII, the Japanese used to camouflage some of their aircraft using bundles of weeds dipped in paint and applied in a distressed pattern. So, how could I get hold of a 90 mm scale weed bundle? Easy, I just took an old, flared brush, cut the bristles with a new surgical blade to obtain a sharp, even cut and scribbled the paint onto the border. I then retouched it here and there to finish it off.

The helmet and vambrances (elbow protectors) were done as follows. Mars black (W & N oils) was first applied and any excess removed. Then, while the paint was still wet, I made that sort of etched design using a burnishing tool made from a chisel-

Step by Step

shaped hypodermic needle. Finally, when everything was dry, the deepest shadows were applied using lampblack, and the final highlights were done by burnishing the edges.

Photos 34 - 53 show the step-by-step treatment of the main body.

TUNIC

Base: yellow ochre
Highlights: base + Naples yellow
Final highlights: highlights + titanium white
Shadows: violet (diluted glaze)

Border of the tunic is 825 (V) violet brown and design blocked in with 856 (V) ochre brown. Highlight is 913 (V) yellow ochre and final highlight is brilliant yellow.

LEATHER JERKIN

Base: 872 (V) chocolate brown
Highlights: orange yellow + titanium white
Shadows: blue black (navy blue + black)

CHEST AND LEG STRAPS

Base: 818 (V) red leather
Highlights: base + raw sienna + titanium white
Shadows: blue black

WAIST SASH

Base: 837 (V) pale sand
Stripes: 846 (V) mahogany brown
Highlights on yellow section: base + titanium white
Highlights on brown section: base + yellow orange
Shadows on the sash were done using burnt umber.

HAT AND NECK COVER HANGING DOWN THE BACK

Hat

Base: Japanese khaki (A)
Highlights: base + titanium white
Shadows: raw umber

The finished base walkaround.

COVER

Base: 803 (V) brown rose
Highlights: base + Naples yellow + titanium white
Shadows: primary red + brilliant green deep

BOOTS

Base: 876 (V) brown sand + raw sienna
Highlights: base + yellow ochre + yellow orange + titanium white
Shadows: burnt sienna

Step by Step

CLOTH AROUND LANCE
Base: primary red
Highlights: base + brilliant red + brilliant yellow
Shadows: black (diluted glaze)

LANCE
Base: wood (A)
Highlights: base + yellow ochre + titanium white
Shadows: black

QUIVER AND SWORD SCABBARD
Base: dark leather (A)
Highlights: base + primary yellow + titanium white + brilliant orange + titanium white
Inner design was painted with 875 beige brown and highlighted with brilliant yellow + titanium white. Shadows were added in blue black.

WAIST BELTS AND SWORD SLINGS
Base: 984 (V) flat brown
Highlights: base + raw sienna + brilliant yellow + titanium white
Shadows: blue black

Oils, as previously described, were used on the remaining metal surfaces.

EPILOGUE
In conclusion, it was a very tedious project although a very rewarding because, as I said at the beginning, it is a gem of a sculpture!! I hope I have done it justice with my paint "splashing."

The base from above.

Germanic Warrior

75 mm
Germanic Warrior: Pegaso (75-024)

Acrylic Colors: Vallejo, Andrea, Life Color
Metallic colors: Testors
Oil paints: Winsor & Newton

DAVIDE DECINA
PHOTOGRAPHS: PAOLO ANTINORI
TEXT ARRANGEMENTS AND PHOTOGRAPHS
CAPTIONS: COSTAS RODOPOULOS

Frontal shot of the entire figure. The many different textures that have to be recreated make this 75 mm figure very interesting for both the painter and the admirer.

The Pegaso 75 mm Germanic Warrior is a classic example of an interesting and demanding figure kit for painters. This is because it offers many different kinds of materials to paint, including metals, leather, fur, skin, cloth, and wood. So, having purchased it, I decided to paint it with the natural colours that the Germanic people from this particular historical period would have probably used, avoiding any outlandish, unnatural colours that would also lose historical accuracy. One suggestion, don't ever use a pure colour when painting an ancient warrior, rather mix them with some other different "strange colour" such as (a) confederate gray, (v) green ochre or (v) salmon rose, etc. In this way, you will get interesting chromatic variations and have many possibilities for shading and highlighting different with tones.

The manufacturers of the colours indicated in the text by an initial are as follows:
(v) = Vallejo, (a) = Andrea's color, (l) = Life color, (t) = Testors

CLOAK

I began the cloak by painting the interior that was made of fur and, as usual, began by using an acrylic color as an undercoat followed by oil colors.

In this instance, I used yellow ochre (v) and then with oil paint washes of burnt sienna and burnt earth, I applied the medium highlights and oil yellow ochre washes for the final highlights. I did the same for the fur around the waist but, for this, I painted the first highlights with acrylics: confederate grey (a), and the final highlights with confederate grey (a) + ice yellow (v). For the exterior, I felt that a red was correct, so I mixed a base color of black (v), basic red (a), Napoleonic green (a), and flat earth (v). For the first highlights, I added more basic red and, for the final highlights, salmon rose (v).

The right side of the figure. Note the carefully toned muscle lining of the hand.

Left side of the figure. The careful highlighting on the fur is evident, giving it a realistic look and adding to the figure's overall realism.

Close-up of the left leg. The leggings must be carefully outlined and highlighted to get the right result

BREECHES

I first made a base mixture of black (v) + Prussian blue (a) + flat earth (v). For the first and second highlights, I added on flat blue (v) and ultramarine (v), and for the final highlights a little confederate grey (a) added to the colour that I used for the second highlights.

The figure's right view, showing the natural colours that are not so vivid, mostly having an "earth" feeling. This is necessary for this particular warrior.

SHIELD

I decided to swap the original kit shield for a round shield that was probably more in keeping with the Germanic tribes of that time. I decided paint it black and yellow. The black was made using a mixture of black (v) + dark flesh (a). For the yellow, I began with a base of black (v) + light orange (v) + violet (v). The highlights were done with yellow ochre (v), which was even used for the final highlights. After drawing two marks of the totemic beast using black (v) + basic red (a), I added the highlights using the basic red. The wood that can be seen on the reverse of the shield was painted with a base of green ochre (v) acrylic, and then the wood grain was done with burnt sienna and burnt earth oil colours. The axe handle was painted in an identical manner.

Close-up of the figure's upper half. All the details, like the jewellery and other smaller items carried by the Germanic Warrior, have been carefully painted to accentuate the total picture of the miniature.

Close-up of the waist area. Note all the overlapping different textures, which must be carefully shaded and highlighted, while also remaining defined and separated.

Close-up on the switched round shield. Note the light graduation of the colour tones

SKIN TONE

All the areas of skin were first given an acrylic base of dark flesh (a). After that, all the work on the skin was done in oils. I began with the shadows done with burnt earth, then, for the first highlights I used burnt sienna and, for the final highlights, a little titanium white.

SILVER-COLORED METALS

All the silver-colored metals were first cleaned with a soft metal brush. I then applied the shadows using Cassel Earth oil paint. The highlights were made with the chrome silver (t).

GOLD OR BRONZE METALS

After applying a base of a mixture of black (v) + gold (v), I added more gold to the base for the first highlights. For the final highlight, I added gloss natural metal (l) to the gold.

LEATHER

All the leatherwork was given a base coat of black (v) + cavalry brown (v). I used the cavalry brown for the first highlights and light brown (v) for the final highlights. After this, all the leather surfaces were given an oil paint wash of burnt sienna. You will notice that this will give it a real look of leather.

The scramasax hilt, made of bone, was given a base of ice yellow (v) and then shaded with burnt earth oil color.

The rear of the figure. Despite the presence of the tree, the figure is clearly visible, and attention must be paid to this factor.

Praefectus Classis, I-II century A.D.
A Roman Naval Officer

This figure represents a Praefectus Classis, a Roman naval officer. The Roman Navy had its principal fleets anchored at the Port of Miseno, north of Naples, to cover the Tirrenian Sea, and at the Port of Classe to cover the Adriatic.

75 mm
Praefectus Classis, I-II century A.C.:
Pegaso Models, "Elite Series" (75-027)
Acrylic Colors: Andrea, Vallejo
Oil paints: Winsor & Newton, Cassel
Primer: Tamiya Grey

PIETRO BALLONI
PHOTOGRAPHS: PEGASO STUDIO

Other fleets where based at certain strategic points around the borders of the Empire. The Britannica, Moesica and Siriana fleets where used for defence of the seas, while the Germanica and Pannonica fleets were used for patrolling the rivers such as the Rhine and Danube.

The principal class of warship was the trireme supported by the liburne, ships of a lighter structure and design.

Warships were distinguished by the color "Veneto" or Sky Blue. According to Vegezio's testimony, the battle standard donated by Augustus to his victorious admiral Agrippa was of a dark blue color.

The soldiers carried aboard the naval vessels were considered to be of inferior rank to the legionaries, even though, in moments of crisis, the Emperor sourced further Legions from these "marines."

The most famous Roman admiral was Marco Vipsanio Agrippa. One of the largest ancient Roman monuments that stands intact today, the Pantheon, was erected by him and displays symbols of the Roman Marines, such as dolphins and tridente, which were sacred symbols of the god Neptune.

THE FIGURE

Pegaso's Praefectus figure was sculpted by the Russian Victor Konnov, who has posed the officer during battle, issuing orders to the sailors with his back close to the trireme's wooden rail. The casting is very crisp, and the parts fit is excellent...there is the added advantage of having the two legs and the torso cast as a single piece. In total, the kit consists of just eight parts for the figure and two for the base. The only minor difficulty is with the cloak as, after gluing, it is necessary to use a small amount of putty to eliminate the join line between the separate parts of the cloak, which has one part cast together with the figure's upper left shoulder.

I would suggest painting the inside of the cloak before gluing it. The outside can be painted later.

PAINTING

As always, I began the painting of the figures with the flesh tones. In the case of the Roman Officer, this meant the face under the helmet and the arms and legs.

The base color for the flesh (painted over the Tamiya Grey Primer spray I normally use as an undercoat) was from the acrylic color range, more precisely Andrea's dark flesh (the old formula that was really matt). This was then painted over the whole of what are the flesh colored surfaces, I then prepared the oil paint mixtures that I normally use for the highlights and shadows.

I always begin with three basic mixtures:
1) Base mixture for the flesh tone: titanium white + light Naples yellow + cadmium medium red.
2) Corrective mixture for the flesh tone: yellow ochre + cadmium red orange (or orange).
3) Base mixture for shadows: Prussian blue + cadmium purple red.

I mixed the three colors of the base mixture with the target color to obtain a kind of light pink flesh tone. To this, I added the corrective mixture (60% yellow ochre and 40% orange) to balance the color into a credible flesh tone.

This is done because flesh tone is not a normal color possessing natural highlights and shadows. Look at yourself in a mirror and you will understand what I mean. So, I try to create a tone that is a balanced mixture between red colors (red, orange, etc.,) and yellow colors (Naples, white, ochre, etc.,)

This final five-color mixture is for the first highlights on the figure. To obtain the first shadow, I take some of this first highlight color and then add a color created by mixing the two components of the shadow base mixture. This color must be dominated by purple, so it is the result of mixing +/- 70% cadmium purple red with 30% Prussian blue.

If I then discover that my shadow mixture (first highlight + shadow base mixture) turns somewhat grey, it means that the Prussian blue has reacted with the titanium white and the light Naples yellow

in the mixture. If this happens, I add more purple to the mixture to balance the color.

When I have my two colors ready, I can start to apply them onto the figure. I separate the face, legs and arms into areas of light or shadow. I consequently put my highlight mixture onto the highlight areas and the shadow one onto the shadow areas, making sure not to mix the colors except at the margins. Then, with a new, soft, clean and perfectly dry brush, I start to blend the margins, and just the margins, until I obtain a smooth transaction between the two colors. I have to be careful not to create chaos and blend without discipline and attention or I will end up with the same color over the whole surface with no separation between highlight and shadow areas. Practicing this technique will ensure better and better results.

After this first pass, I have all the acrylic base covered with oil paints and I can start to work separately on the highlights and the shadows (exactly as with acrylic...) putting more titanium white and Naples yellow on the highlights and more of the pure base shadow mixture onto the shadows...

The contrast between the highlights and the shadows is up to you...the only important thing is to make sure the shadows are correct. Only these help the eye to correctly perceive the figure's volumes. Why not try to take time to examine other modellers figures and look at the level of deep shadows the painters have used on particular figures, this is the way to get better.

If my contrasts between light and dark colors are too deep and I am unable to succesfully blend the colors, I use the corrective tone as a semi-tone to help to create a less deep contrast and to make the blending easier. The corrective tone will help (by mixing it on the palette or by applying it directly to the figure and then blending it) when the flesh color is too pink and unrealistic.

Pay close attention when defining the eyes, the nose apertures and the interior of the mouth with its deep shadows as these will help to bring the face "into focus." The lips are painted after adding a little red to the base flesh mixture. When doing this, do it with a light hand or your naval officer will look like a female!

The cuirass is painted with metallic printers' ink mixed, with oil colors for the shadows. I normally use Cassel Earth mixed with the metals, and pure gold printers' ink (or gold mixed with silver) for the highlights. The procedure for painting highlights and shadows and then blend them is exactly the same as for the face, and remains the same for all the items you paint in oils.

The fringes were painted white, but as it is natural leather painted white, this effect has to be created by mixing some earth colors (brown and grey, ochre, Naples yellow) to the white to create a "dirty white" and also to use a very small amount of Linseed oil with the color to get a final effect that is satin and not matt.

A small trick you when painting a figure that consists of many parts that are to represent different materials, but painted with the same color, is to create minor differences in the colors. In the case of our officer, the tunic and cloak are made from blue textiles, the "Pteruges" and "Balteus" are blue leather, there is a blue brush-shaped crest on the helmet and a blue cover on the shield. So, we must use different basic blues and create small differences in the mixtures, for example, the "Pteruges" and the "Balteus" were both painted with oils and more white used on the highlights, the cloak was painted in a very dark blue, then given a first pass with blue oil paints and, finally, completed with the use if powdered pigment applied with a clean, dry brush (don't forget not to touch the cloak after using the powders).

The shield was painted after adding more green tones to the base mixture to obtain an Aquamarine final shade, but small rather than great differences with the rest of the figure.

The shield designs are all hand drawn. Do not be afraid to make a few drafts, it is mostly a question of practice. After making a draft, you then have to convert the draft into a series of geometrical shapes that will assist you to get the correct proportions and symmetry. For example, the design on our Naval Officer's shield is a Triton spear and four dolphins. So, first divide the shield into two vertical parts, divided by the Triton spear, and then and horizontally through the other decoration. There is now symmetry for the dolphins and we can consider the step-by-step method of completing each one of the four parts.

Next, draw draft the balls in the dolphins' mouths. Then, begin to draw the dolphins by measuring the distances that dolphins have to be from the Triton spear, drawing the vertical plane first then the eyes, curves, and the fine detail. This is done step-by-step using a pencil, attempting fix the most important points, and not to draw the whole of the dolphins with all their details, this will be done later using the paint brush. What is important is to establish the basoc volumes.

With this type of work, much like many others, practice makes perfect!

The boots were, of course, painted black, using oil paints. The system for blending the highlights and shadows is the same as mentioned above. What we want to consider is to create a "dirty black" by using warm greys, ochres, Naples yellow mixed to pure black but without losing a final black effect. In fact, when painting black, the most common error is to overdo the highlights and to end up with a grey final effect. When this happens to me, I normally apply an overall oil wash to get the piece back to a darker color.

THE BASE

The base was divided into two parts, the first being the pavement painted with an acrylic undercoat and then with oil paints for lights and shadows. Using different oil paints, it is easy to paint the lines that give the appearance of wood grain. I usually start with a a light wood color for the base, then give it a dark brown oil wash over the whole surface. I then begin to paint the wood grain using medium brown, yellow ochre, flat earth and red brown. Sometimes, I pass a clean brush over the whole surface to blend (but not completely!) these wood grain lines.

The vertical part of the base is painted using the same system as for the pavement, but I tried to create a ruined varnished wood effect. This meant that, after painting the whole surface in wood effect, I then painted the wood with acrylic blue washes followed by blue oil paints to realistically blend the blue painting with the wood texture. In some areas, to obtain a better blending effect, I also painted some typical wood texture (irregular lines on the surface...) but this time using blue oil paints.

Step by Step

PRAETORIAN CENTURION

As has come to be expected from this Italian company, this is a beautifully sculpted 75 mm figure by Pegaso Models. It is of a Praetorian Centurion and, during the assembly and painting of this superb figure I followed the kit instructions and colour chart.

75 mm
Praetorian Centurion: Pegaso (75-029)
Acrylic colors: Maimeri, Andrea
Oil paints: Winsor & Newton

TEXT – PHOTOGRAPHS: RAY FARRUGIA

The completed figure.

After the usual job of cleaning up the parts, and I left the right arm holding the sword, left forearm holding the cloak, and scabbard as sub-assemblies.

As always, I began with the face. So, as in this instance I wanted to depict a European, I used the newly acquired Maimeri tube acrylics throughout unless otherwise specified.

PAINTING
Face
Base color: raw sienna + primary red + burnt sienna + deep yellow + Navy blue (just a touch!)
First highlights: base + deep yellow + flesh
Final highlights: Naples yellow + flesh
First shadows: violet (diluted glaze)
Final shadows: black + primary red
Beard area: Navy blue (diluted glaze)

Helmet
Base: flat brown 984
Highlights: base + red ochre
Shadows: blue black (Navy blue + black)

The decorations on the embossed laurel wreath, the scorpion symbols on the paragnatidi (cheek guards), and the crest were painted with silver printers' ink. The plume was painted in flat red, highlighted with carmine + vermillion hue. The shadows were done using brilliant green deep.

The same leather mix was used for the Lorica (cuirass).

Sagum (Cloak)
Base: black + primary red (reddish brown mix)
Highlights: base + ochre (Andrea)
Shadows: Black

Pteruges (Leather strips on the shoulders and legs)

Base: Cavalry brown 982 + flat red 857
Highlights: base + orange yellow
Shadows: black

Lrather wrist band and sandals

Base: leather brown 871
Highlights: beige brown 875 + medium mesh 860
Shadows: Violet

Tunic

Base: basic red (Andrea) + Napoleonic red (Andrea)
Highlights: base + vermillion hue + brilliant red
High highlights: highlights + flesh
Shadows: brilliant deep green (diluted glaze)

I decided to paint the sword hilt as ivory, so that it would not look all gold! So, I painted it with Ivory 918, highlighted with titanium white and shaded with Van Dyke brown. The sword blade was weathered using lamp black (Winsor & Newton Oils).

The Cnemides (shin guards) were painted with gold printers ink and then shaded with burnt umber (Winsor & Newton Oils).

Finally, what a pleasure it was to paint such a masterpiece. I would like to express my sincere thanks to Stelios Demiras for asking that eternal gentleman, Luca Marchetti of Pegaso Models, to donate an example of this fantastic figure so that I could "splash" on the paint!!

Step by Step

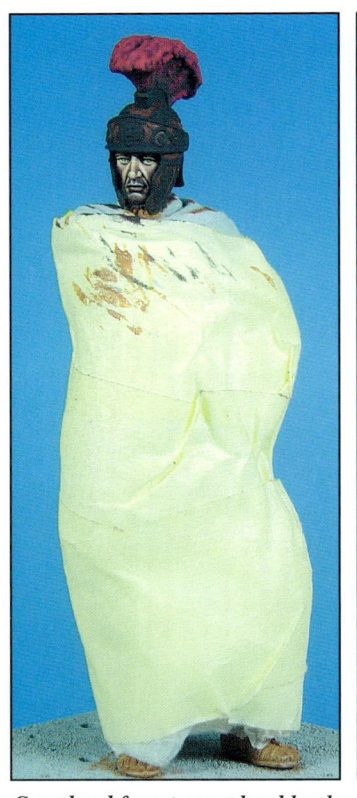 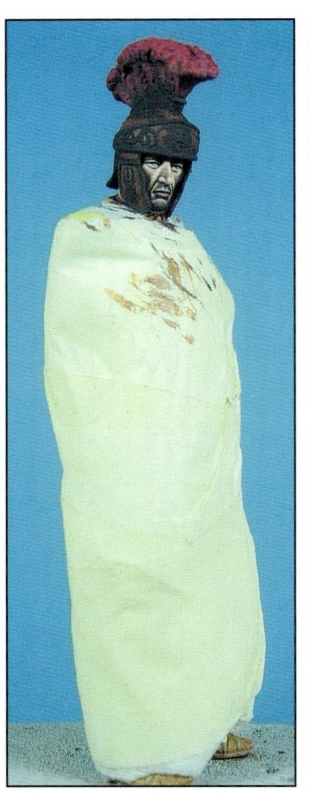 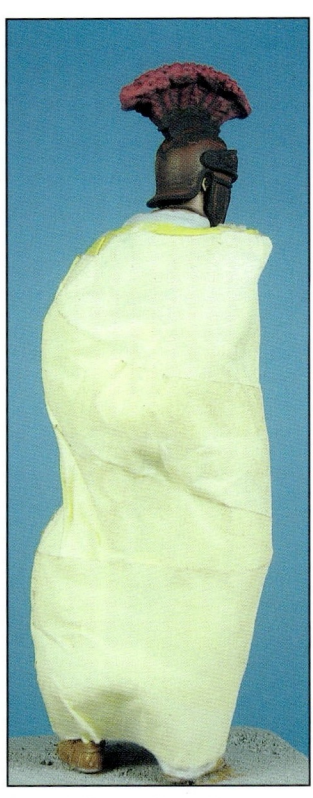 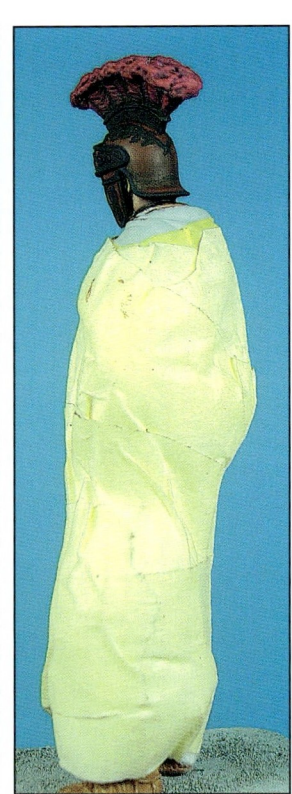

Completed face + completed leather helmet + completed plume + embossed decorations given a coat of base color.

  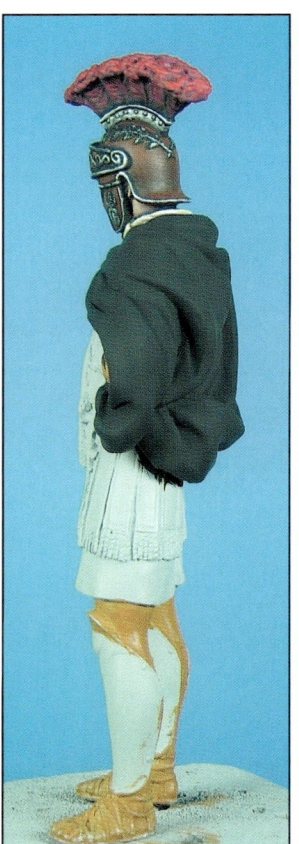 

Completed helmet + cloak (sagum) given a coat of base color.

    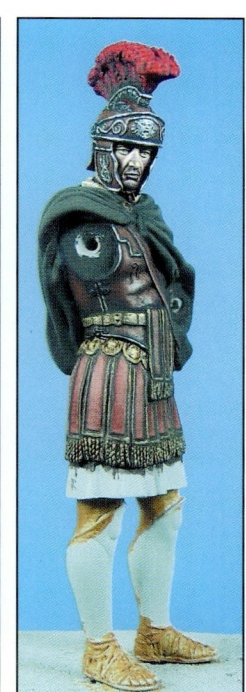

Completed cloak + completed cuirass (lorica) & pteruges.

Competed tunic + shin guards (cnemides) given a coat of base color.

Step by Step

Completed left hand holding folded cloak.

Completed right arm + completed sword.

Completed scabbard.

The finished figure.

Attila and the Black Huns' Empire

Text - historical presentation - illustration and original representation of uniforms: Christos Giannopoulos

The escalation of the barbarian peoples' great migration underlined the impotence of both the Western and Eastern Roman Empires to defend their extended borders against more and more invaders who were encroaching along the Danube. Centuries before the appearance of Genghis Khan, another leader with Turkish-Mongol features became the synonym of absolute depredation, slaughter and all the eschatological predictions concerning the end of the world: Attila, "the Scourge of God," the pre-eminent ruler of the black (western) Huns and Overlord of the Ostrogoths, the Gepids, the Alans and all the other Iranian speaking nomads along the Danube and the Eurasian steppe.

Of course, the image of Attila and the western Huns was created from the nightmares and prejudices of the historians of the bourgeois Mediterranean. These considered the filthy, primeval mounted nomads of the east as a decayed hybrid of human evolution that fed on the corpse of civilisation. For every cultivated citizen of the Roman Empire, there existed barbarians who challenged the disciplined legions and were creatures forgotten since the dawn of time.

Attila's Huns, however, were something even worse: unsightly demons debouching from Darkness and Chaos, which pre-existed the dawn of time. Their slit eyes, prominent cheekbones, their deliberately knife - slashed faces (a bizarre manifestation of beautification and sign of masculinity for the Huns) and their strange hairstyle, were in sharp contrast with the ancient Greco-Roman ideal of beauty or Christian morality that had been adopted by both the Western and Eastern Roman Empires.

The Huns would probably have remained just an occasional threat if Attila had not united them in 445 A.D. and established the first barbarian empire, which stood against both Rome and China simultaneously. The western civilisation had suffered raids, humiliation and countless provocation for around eight years resulting in the macabre setting of devastated cities, strewn with slaughtered inhabitants devoured by packs of stray dogs. It is, indeed, a parody for the urban civilisation that Attila's armies included Roman deserters besides other barbarian nations. It is rumoured that his closest confidante and consultant was Orestes, a Greek deserter who dreamt of seeing his son an emperor in the ruins of Rome. Attila's ambitions came to an end in 451 A.D., at the Battle of the Plains of Chalons in Gaul, when his multinational army confronted an equally powerful military coalition consisting of Romans, Romanised Celts from Gaul and Britain, Franks and Visigoths, under the leadership of Flavius Aetius, a Roman general of barbarian background that had grown up with the Huns. The bloody battle resulted in Attila's flight with the remnants of his army, a flight seconded by Flavius Aetius' mysterious tolerance. Attila would return once again, this time ravaging Italy, (although, this time, his army halted its advance at the suburbs of Rome). Attila's meeting with the Pope would be long committed to Italian memory, as the Hun leader's retreat following their – largely unrecorded – conversation was considered a miracle.

In 453 A.D., the great "Hagan" of the western Huns died under mysterious circumstances and his empire broke apart due to domestic infighting. Flavius Aetius, the victor of the Battle of the Plains of Chalons, was murdered in the middle of political conspiracies, extremely common during that historical period, while the Western Roman Empire was officially annihilated in 476 A.D. by new swarms of barbarians led by warlords, formerly officers of the Roman army. The Eastern Roman Empire, widely known as the Byzantine Empire, would survive for another thousand years, until it, in its turn, fell pieces as a result of internecine battles and pressure from the probable descendants of the Huns, the Turks.

ATTILA. There is insufficient information or evidence pertaining to Attila's military dress, so this illustration is primarily based on archaeological material discovered about the Huns, dated circa 5th century A.D. Attila's copper-plated helmet is the original Hun spagenhelm with extended nasal – bar and Mongolian style – pseudo Roman crest, a reminder of his imperial ambitions. The impressive, full body armor, is of the Turranic type "Tarkan," and consists of iron plates, covered externally with bronze, while from the gilded waist belt, hangs the typical Hun dagger with a ring shaped pommel, and a long cavalry sword. His hand protection consists of metal plates, while he carries additional chain mail armor of the "Cupe Yarik" type (an armor type, more common to the era's Huns of Eastern Europe and Iran than to the same tribal residents of Mongolia and China. The King of the Huns emblem was the golden bow, that Attila is shown holding in his right hand. (uniform research and reconstruction by Christos Giannopoulos)

HUN RIDER. *This illustration of a cavalry warrior represents a member of the mounted aristocracy of the "Black Huns" that advanced into Russia during the 3rd Century A.D. He wears the famous "Phrygian" cap of the nomadic tribes of the Eurasian prairies, full body armor of the "Say Yarik" type made from lacquered leather plates, a complex bow, hourglass-shaped quiver, and a double cut Turranic sword, with cross-shaped hilt. The horse has leather armor protection. (uniform research and reconstruction by Christos Giannopoulos)*

OSTROGOTH WARLORD. *This illustration represents the appearance of a Goth aristocratic cavalryman from the Crimea that took part in Attila's campaigns. Note the compilation of Germanic, Roman and Asian characteristics: Golden bracelet, curved sword, wide leather belt, spear, and the flat round shield of the cavalry warrior are the Germanic elements of his appearance, the matching of a red cloak and chain mail armor, following the era's style of Roman cavalry dress, while the use of a complex cuirass, with half-lamellar parts, and the voluminous trousers, are distinctive elements of Iranian influence. (uniform research and reconstruction by Christos Giannopoulos)*

ROMAN CAVALRY OFFICER. *The officer illustrated here represents the few Mediterranean army officers, of the East and West Roman Empire. He wears a heavy "Cassis" type helmet – a bad copy of earlier prototypes of the classic headgear, a short iron thorax – also a reminder of earlier periods – articulated iron armor as hand and knee protectors, an ellipsoid shield decorated with the Christian symbol "XP", a heavy cavalry spear (Lancea) and a long double cut sword (Spatha Equitata). (uniform research and reconstruction by Christos Giannopoulos)*

RED HUN. This specific illustration represents the anthropological characteristics and the dress code of the Huns that settled in Iran and Afghanistan and mixed with the local races. The warrior presented here s shown clad in the equipment of a King's bodyguard: short chain mail armor, with added chain mail sleeves, a complex helmet (spagenhelm) manufactured by Iranian craftsmen, with additional chain mail neck protector, dark-colored tunic with decorations of Central Asia origin, an Iranian-style round shield, an Afghan style iron mace – suitable for close combats – and leather knee protectors decorated with hawks (the Huns sacred symbol). The only original Hun element is the horizontal hanging dagger with a ring-shaped pommel. (uniform research and reconstruction by Christos Giannopoulos)

VISIGOTH FOOT WARRIOR. In contrast to the Ostrogoths, the Visigoths that ruled in Germany and France paid much more attention to the use of infantry. The warrior illustrated here carries a large, human shaped, shield, with leather frame, a large "Seax" type machete, a "West Baltic" type spear, a pike with leaf shaped edge, and a highly penetrating pike of "Angon" type. The heavy double cut sword (not shown here) completed the offensive arms of these foot soldiers. Formed into dense formations of highly disciplined, energetic warriors, the Visigoth infantry were able to defeat any Roman Legion and face any cavalry unit. (uniform research and reconstruction by Christos Giannopoulos)

Templar Sergeant
XIII Century - The Villain

90 mm
Templar Sergeant, XIII Century: Pegaso (90-038)
Acrylic Colors: Vallejo, Andrea, Life Color
Metallic colors: Testors
Oil paints: Winsor & Newton

DAVIDE DECINA
PHOTOGRAPHS: PAOLO ANTINORI
TEXT ARRANGEMENTS AND PHOTOGRAPH CAPTIONS: COSTAS RODOPOULOS

Pegaso's 90 mm. "Templar Knight" is, in my humble opinion, one of the most impressive miniatures ever released. After seeing the figure, I thought that it might be a good idea to paint it as a knight in dark colours. After talking to my friend, Marco Giuliani, who is an expert on the Middle Ages, he suggested that would be very interesting to paint a black scorpion on a red background on the shield as an heraldic device. Why? Because, during the Middle Ages, this was a symbol for evil and thus it was perfect for the particular figure I had in mind. As for the tunic, we thought that it would also be good to use a black base on which many small orange/red eagles were sewn. So to the cloak and we came up with the idea of using black for the exterior and a very dark yellow for the lining.

The colors used are indicated in the text along with the particular brand's initial letter as follows:
(v) = Vallejo
(a) = Andrea's color
(l) = Life color
(t) = Testors

SHIELD

Base: black (v) + basic red (a), leaning toward a rather dark color and not a very vivid color mix. For the first highlights, I added a little more basic red to the base or you could also use just basic red. For the final highlights, use basic red (a) + Napoleonic red (a). The scorpion has a base of black, with a mixture of black (v) + dark flesh (a) for the highlights.

The shield's metal fittings were painted with a mixture of black (v) + gloss natural metal (l) for the base to give a gun metal shade, then add some more gloss natural metal for the first highlights. For the final highlights, use chrome silver (t). The wooden interior of the shield was given a base coat of green ochre (v). After that, I used oil colours, burnt umber and burnt sienna, for the wood grain pattern.

CLOAK

The base color for the outer surface was black (v), with a mixture of black (v) + dark flesh (a)

Every detail of the figure must be carefully toned individually to achieve the desired overall result.

The long cloak requires good planning during the painting and, of course, much patience and careful brushwork.

A 90mm figure always requires a lot of work and patience especially if you intend to do a lot of repeat designs on the tunic, as with this one.

for the highlights. For the top of the cloak, I used a little flat earth (v) to recreate the textile effect. The base for the inside was made of black (v) + violet (v) + light orange (v) to obtain a strange, dark color! For the first highlights, a little orange followed by yellow ochre (v) was used. A little golden yellow (v) was used for the final highlights.

TUNIC

The exterior was painted with the same colours as the cloak, except for the flat earth. The interior was painted with violet (v) + black (v). For the highlights, I added a little violet (v) while, for the final highlights, confederate grey (a). For the heraldry i.e. the eagles, I began with cavalry brown (v), for the first highlights I added Napoleonic red (a) + cavalry brown (v), and the final highlight a little light orange (v).

SHIRT BENEATH THE TUNIC

The base was made using black (v) + basic red (a) + Napoleonic green (a). For the highlights, I gradually increased the amount of basic red to the base colour.

Front left view of the figure, where the gradually muted color of the tunic designs is evident as we go down closer to the ground.

The rear of the figure. Note how impressive the large shield looks hanging on the knight's back. Also, how the long cloak compliments the shield.

LEATHERS, BOOTS AND GLOVES

The base was cavalry brown (v) + green ochre (v) + black (v). I then used the same oil colors as for the wood but with the addition of oil yellow ochre for the final highlights.

FACE

I always begin a face with an acrylic base of dark flesh (a) and then use a mixture of oil colours, burnt sienna, burnt umber and titanium white, to complete it. By using these shades, all the different variations of skin tone, starting by the shadows and ending with the highlights, can be accomplished.

STEEL CHAINMAIL AND SWORD

After cleaning all the metal parts with a soft metal brush, Cassel Earth oil color was used for the shadows, while the highlights were done with Testors chrome silver.

After completing the painting, using a soft dry brush, I added some earth pigments colours to give the figure a realistic dusty look.

And...there it was! With lots of patience, this amazing sculpture can be painted as any knight from the first half of the XIII century. The end result is will definitely satisfy the painter.

The shield with the scorpion design across the knight's back.

Right side of the figure, showing the careful shading and highlighting of all the different areas of the figure.

Byzantine Imperial
Cavalry Standard-bearer (13th-14th century A.D.)

TEXT-PHOTOGRAPHS: COSTAS RODOPOULOS

Another view showing the steepness of the ground, as well as the intense shading on both figures.

Rider figure: PEGASO 75 – 041 "Byzantium Standard Bearer – 12th -14th century A.D."
Horse figure: From the kit (SH75016) by Seil Models "Templar Knight"

Acrylic colors: Andrea, Vallejo
Alcohol based colors (metallic): Kokolo Adithes, Vallejo
Oil paints: Maimeri, W&N, Talens Pro Series
Brushes: W&N, Da Vinci, Leonardo
Printer's ink: Best Soldiers by Marco Changhini
Scenery - Base: Wooden base (7.5 x 7.5 cm) from La Meridiana, natural stones from Nayplion
Epoxy putty for conversion - sculpting: Magic Sculp, Duro
Epoxy glue (2 parts): Araldite 90 seconds cure

HISTORICAL INFORMATION

The primary result of the 4th Crusade in the Hellenic region was the breakdown of stability and security that the Byzantine Empire had, until then, guaranteed. After the Crusader attack on Constantinople, the many ambitions for creating small independent kingdoms surfaced. The Bulgarian threat to capture land in the Macedonian region was an additional factor for instability.

As this situation progressed, many smaller Byzantine and Latin states were created in the Aegean area as well as in Asia Minor, breaking forever the unifying influence of the Byzantine Empire. The most important of these smaller states were the Constantinople Empire and the Latin Kingdom of Thessaloniki, Attica and Viotia, as well as Peloponnese.

Many civil wars broke out, with ensuing disastrous results, leaving the way open for the Ottomans to take advantage of the situation. They mounted raids and captured fortresses in the area of Thrace.

On the 29th of May 1453 A.D., the Turkish army under Mohamed II conquered

The completed figure in a snowy setting looks impressive. The superb sculpting of Andrea Jula, along with the conversion, imparts to the miniature a sense of authority.

The figure, before final polishing and after the sculpting of the fur has been completed. Other parts, like the arms and sword are attached with Blue Tack for test fitting purposes. The broken standard and the remaining part can be seen on the right wrist.

The left side of the almost completed converted figure, showing the fur edging around the cloak. The repositioned arrow case can also be seen temporarily attached to its locating pin to test it for fit and correct positioning.

Constantinople. During the battle, Konstantin Paleologos, the last of the Byzantine emperors, was killed and thus ended the glorious Byzantine Empire that had lasted for over 1000 years.

THE FIGURES

This vignette is based on the wonderful Pegaso Models figure of the "Byzantine Standard Bearer – 12th-14th century A.D." figure (Kit No: 75-041), sculpted by the talented Andrea Jula. It was inspired (as mentioned in the kit's explanatory texts) on the magnificent illustration of Byzantine Cavalry by Christos Giannopoulos. This artwork is featured on the cover of the influential book "Byzantine Army" - The Guardian of the 1000 Years Empire," published by Periscopio Publications, (www.periscopio.gr)

The artwork is itself based on historical information gleaned from the 14th century A.D. Byzantine manuscript entitled 'History of Alexander the Great'. The basic items of clothing used on the Pegaso figure are the scale armor, chain mail, leather chest bands, and all decorations including the imperial eagle and the crosses.

The horse is a conversion of the Knight Templar horse that is part of the Seil Models kit No: SH75016. (Seil Models, unfortunately, recently ceased operations)

ASSEMBLY – CONVERTING THE STANDARD BEARER

The quality of Pegaso Models kits is always the best, especially in the larger scales like 75 mm or 90 mm. This figure is no exception! In fact, it is one of the finest figures I have ever painted. The sculpting is about perfect with the resultant cleaning up minimal (just a few fine mould lines, and these not in critical places). I polished the figure using a bronze brush in a power tool (avoiding the chain mail to avoid any possible damage).

The horse, after a lot of time spent converting it, almost ready for priming. As can be seen, 99% of the rebuilding – conversion was done with lead foil. It was more suitable for the purpose than putty. I required many linear objects and it was no use trying to sculpt them.

The figure's right side, the fur edging around the cloak is clearly visible, also the twisted, metal part of the cloak (after the interior had been greatly thinned down to make it curve around the Standard Bearer's body). A number of marks caused by the work carried out to stretch it are still evident. They were easily eliminated during the final polishing.

A rear shot of the reworked horse reveals shows all metal parts used and the extra decoration on the saddle. The extensive use of epoxy putty to make the base is also evident.

Metal pins were inserted for attaching the right arm, which was then test fitted until it sat exactly right, mainly because the weight of the standard would place a lot of pressure on that joint via the wrist. The left arm was also pinned to hold it securely under its own weight. However, this arm could not be attached prior to painting, as it would get in the way during the subsequent painting process. The plans for the figure's conversion included transferring the arrow case to the left side of the waist, and this was also secured with a pin. Many test fittings were also carried here, because of the short distance between the arm and the case.

On the top of the left wrist was a hole to accept the shield. However, as I had already decided to hang the shield on the horse's saddle, this hole was filled and the top of the hand re-sculpted with putty.

While making the original studies for the conversion, and given that the horse's saddle cloth had a natural wind blown movement to the left (as the observer looks at the scene), the planned rider's cloak (this was an addition inspired by the painting by Thanos Vassilikos for cover of the book titled "Byzantine – Bulgarian wars" by Periscopio Publications) also had to move to the left.

Having started to prepare the pattern for the rider's cloak, I noticed that the Knight Templar in the Seil kit had a cloak that was also blowing in the breeze and in the right direction. Utilizing this would be a lifesaver, if I was lucky enough and the part could be adapted to the Byzantine figure's

A side view of the horse on the base, showing all the added detail. The acutely angled base was used to add drama to the scene.

A crucial point of the whole procedure...test fitting the two figures to the base. The distance between them is so small that everything had to be double checked before beginning to paint. As hoped, the initial planning was correct and everything worked out just fine! Notice the symmetry of the cloak, and the horse cloth flowing in the same direction.

shoulder area, as it would save me a lot of sculpting work and time. However, it was not to be and, although I could use the Templar's cloak, it was still going to require a lot of work to adapt it to my figure!

Although to two figures were to the same scale (!) their body dimensions were significantly different. So, using a motor tool, different files, a scalpel with fresh blades, and different pairs of flat-nosed pliers, I began to remove material from the inside of the cloak, filing and cutting, and also bending the part, to make it fit the body of my figure. While doing this, I had to do make many test fittings, as I had to take care so that the completed cloak did not get in the way of the two, and would also leave enough space for the arrow case. After working on it for two complete evenings, I got the result I was after.

After attaching the cloak, the figure began to look like a high-ranking officer so I decided to add some fur edging around it. In addition, the fur would also add weight to impression of winter that I wanted to achieve. For the fur, I used a mixture of 40% Magic Sculp and 60% Duro (Green Stuff) and rolled out a "snake." I began by gluing small lengths of this, using CA glue, around the edge of the cloak and sculpting the fur texture at the same time. The sculpting was done using a fresh, wet scalpel blade and brass rods that had been filed to a sharp point.

Adding and sculpting the fur took two afternoons to complete. Making fur requires attention, first making sure it follows the general direction of the way animal hair lies, but also including some small, local imperfections to add realism. A lot of attention was paid around the shoulder areas, so that the fur ending would be symmetrical, as well as on the chest area, where I made a small cavity for a metal buckle button that I inserted afterwards.

While cleaning up the standard, which was not to be converted, the law of impatience confirmed its existence. Despite following the "standard cleaning procedure" using a scalpel, files and sandpaper, I also used the motor tool fitted with a wire brush. In an instant of carelessness, the motor tool spoiled the

A rear view of the vignette, showing the scene's tight composition, with the whole setting on a square base of just 7.5 cm.

PAINTING THE FIGURE

Flesh
Base: 927 dark flesh + 944 old rose + 981 orange brown + 921 English uniform + 955 flat flesh + 812 violet red
Highlights: base + 955 flat flesh + 928 light flesh
Shadows: base + 921 + 814 burnt cadmium red

Beard
Base: 877 gold brown + 856 ochre brown + 981 orange brown
Highlights: base + 911 light orange + 915 deep yellow + 806 German yellow
Shadows: base + 856 + 941 burnt umber + 862 black gray

Helmet
The helmet's metal surface was first burnished and then given 3 coats of diluted Tamiya smoke. The highlights where done with silver printer's ink and the shadows with diluted Cassel earth oil paint. A further coat of Tamiya smoke was then applied. A few more highlights where applied using printer's ink. All the gold detailing on the helmet was painted with golden printer's ink.

Scale armor
Base: 998 bronze + 878 old gold
Highlights: Adithes old gold + 849 super gold + 796 white gold
Shadows: Tamiya smoke + wash with Cassel earth + lamb black oil paint

Any tonal variations were created using different mixtures of metallic colors to specific scale armor flakes.

part and it ended up in four pieces that were, of course, quite useless. After calming my panic, I decided that this was not so bad as I could still always use the remaining decoration on the standard for the horse I planned on using. However, I now had to find another standard, and this I cajoled a good friend into giving me from his kit. This time I cleaned it with patience and normal procedure, encountering no further problems.

The figure was then primed with Vallejo white spray primer and left to dry for 48 hours.

Even after priming, I continued to test fit it and removed all traces of primer from the pins to ensure an initial tight assembly.

The figure was then secured to the aluminium painting grip and I was then ready to start...

Most of the areas requiring metallic colors have been completed, even though they are part of different areas of the model. I prefer to do this as I have had the experience of finishing a well-painted area only for it to subsequently become dirtied with metallic printer's ink. So, I try to avoid this as much as possible. During this stage, the figure begins to reveal some character.

The painting of the face is close to 90% complete. To save time, I usually do parallel work. While painting the face, I also worked on the helmet and the first stages of the flake armor. Note the primed fur. I try to keep other parts free of paint while working because sometimes it's hard to eliminate careless brushstrokes, which results in extra, unnecessary work.

In this close-up shot can be seen what the lead foil flakes look like after being made and prior to being used. I use strips of lead foil, which can be found in art shops, as it's thinner and easier to manipulate. I made over 1.400 flakes, although not all of them were a success and couldn't be used. Here are some of the remaining ones.

This is my punch-and-die set that I purchased from a jewelry supply store. It has many different diameters suitable for all purposes and cost around 60 Euros. However, as the quality is so good, they can also be used for punching out circular pieces for shields, decoration, scenery, etc., I really feel that it was a good investment.

Chain Mail
Base: 865 oily steel + 861 glossy black
Highlights: Base + silver printer's ink
Shadows: Cassel earth oil paint + wash using black oil paint

Red Cloth
Base: 957 flat red + 829 purpleheart red + 908 carmine red
Highlights: Base + 851 deep orange + 805 German orange
Shadows: Base + 814 burnt cadmium red

Beige Trousers
Base: 820 off white + 872 chocolate brown
Highlights: Base + 918 ivory + 820 off white
Shadows: Base + 872

Purple Cloak and Knee Decorations (with slight tonal differences)
Base: 810 royal purple + 950 black + 960 violet + 811 blue violet
Highlights: permanent red/violet + white oil paint
Shadows: permanent red/violet + Cassel earth + black oil paint

Cloak Fur
Base: 950 black + 836 London gray + 870 medium sea gray
Highlights: base + 883 silver gray + white oil paint
Shadows: 822 German camouflage black brown + 862 black gray + wash with Cassel earth + diluted black oil paint

Red Leather Boots
Base: 926 red + 946 dark red + 829 amaranth red
Highlights: base + 910 orange red + 911 light orange
Shadows: Cassel earth + black oil paint

Arrow Case - Leather Chest Strap
Base: 810 royal purple + 811 blue violet
Highlights: permanent red/violet + white oil paint
Shadows: permanent red/violet + Cassel earth oil paint

Sword Scabbard
Base: 946 dark red + 829 amaranth red
Highlights: base + 910 orange red + 911 light orange
Shadows: Cassel earth oil paint

Leather Waist Belt
Base: 941 burnt umber + 950 black
Highlights: base + 836 London gray + 883 silver gray
Shadows: Cassel earth oil paint

White Metal Armor
Base: 863 gunmetal grey + 865 oily steel + 861 glossy black
Highlights: silver printers ink
Shadows: Tamiya smoke + wash with diluted Cassel earth and black oil paint

A close-up of the Standard-bearer. During the painting procedure, as there were many metal surfaces to paint, I tried to get a shine on the metal although being careful not to overdo it. I also tried to take advantage of the perfect sculpting of the scale armor, with accentuating each and every flake. I achieved this with tonal variations of the metal color.

To paint the cloak was a real challenge! I wanted an impressive imperial purple color, while also giving it intense contrast that was justified by the natural movement of the cloak. Note also the painting of the fur to give it depth.

Metallic Gold for Chest Strap Decoration, knee protectors and standard Decorations

Gold printers ink + wash of Cassel earth oil paint + one coat of Tamiya smoke
Highlights: a mixture of silver and gold printer's ink

Standard (Red Cloth)

Base: 926 red + 946 dark red + 980 black green
Highlights: base + 910 orange red
Shadows: Cassel earth + black oil paint

Standard (Wooden Shaft)

Base: 846 mahogany brown + 829 amaranth red + 877 gold brown
Highlights: base + 860 medium flesh tone + 948 golden yellow
Shadows: Cassel earth + black oil paint

Standard design

Base: AC-51 (Andrea) golden ochre + 948 golden yellow + a little 996 gold
Highlights: base + 806 German yellow + 858 ice yellow + 918 ivory
Shadows: base + 941 burnt umber + 856 ochre brown

HORSE

For the horse, I used the one from the Seil Models kit (SH75016, although now, unfortunately, out of production) of the Knight Templar. This offered a horse, as the pose was somewhat static, the model was not really "loaded", and I thought it would be easy enough to convert it to what I wanted.

First, I cleaned it carefully, using a scalpel, files, a motor tool with wire brush, and sand paper, and then was assembled it using Araldite epoxy glue. Next, any imperfections, especially around the belly area, were filled with putty and sanded smooth.

With regard to the construction of the scale armor, the plan was to first make a pattern from lead sheet, so I could ensure perfect symmetry on both sides. Then, using fresh Magic Sculp putty, fix

This view shows the deep shading of the arrow case, this is justified because it is partly hidden under the soldier's arm and cloak. Note how the shading of the scale armor continues in the same direction when passing under the chain mail. It is vitally important to take into account when shading and highlighting miniatures that they are part of a whole and not doing them as individual items.

A side view of the rear of the horse, giving a full-on view of the shield. The shape, and standard of sculpting made it easy to paint and add the designs. Transferring the shield and bow case onto the horse maintained an overall balance against the other supplementary pieces of the standard bearer's equipment.

the flakes one by one. The flakes would also be made of lead sheet. However, this plan could not be carried out immediately as the 'waving' of the saddlecloth would not allow me to layer the armor base properly.

In consequence, with the use of the power tool fitted with a sanding bit, most of the folds in the cloth were eliminated, leaving a much smoother area that allowed the armor base to be layered. To smooth the area, I first polished it with a wire brush and the power tool.

Then the sections of the pattern, 3 for each side, were measured and cut from thin lead sheet. The intermediate part had to be completed before the final positioning, while the front and back, because of the size and difficulty, would be glued to the horse and the flakes added.

The larger front and rear parts of the lead sheet armor base were glued on with epoxy glue and left to dry. At the same time, positioning the flakes on the two smaller belly triangles began. For creating the armor flakes, a punch and die system was used over lead sheet. Without using much force and applying a sharp, controlled tap, the flakes were punched out and then used. They were each lifted out with the wet tip of a brush and positioned on the correct spot, adjusting them finally with the brush and toothpick.

Creating flake armor in this way requires patience, time and to remain calm. It is also needs to be carried out at a good working speed, as the fresh putty will begin to cure, making the positioning of the flakes harder. To avoid this, it is best to work in small sections, starting from the lower end and proceeding higher. In you need to stop the operation for any reason, this will not cause any problem.

After many hours of repetitive work, and the application of over 1.130 flakes, with many others discarded (along with an accidentally broken horse ear, re-sculpted with Duro as it disappeared into thin air!), making the armor was completed, and

A side view of the horse, showing all the detail work and the decoration, as well as the positioning of the bow case on the saddle. To fill this area, and have the rider dismounted, the cloak was added so that there was no space for one more piece of equipment.

A rear view, this is dominated by the impressive purple colored cloak with its high contrasts around the folds. Painting it in this way enhances the cloak's sense of movement.

left to completely dry to avoid any of the flakes detaching while being painted.

Once again using lead sheet, the horse's reins and all the other leather straps were cut, as well as the metal plates down the centre line of horse. Also, the decorations on the fore head were added after all were test fitted to ensure a perfect fit. Some decorative improvements were done on the saddle, and all these small parts were checked one by one to ensure the attachments were secure to avoid any accidents during painting or later.

All areas were then cleaned of any remains of glue or putty.

With this, the, by now, very heavy horse was ready, and it and the rider were test fitted to the base, both before and after priming. As the space between the two figures was very small, extensive test fitting had to be done to avoid any surprises later on. This, of course, meant that extra care had to be taken when the time came to finally position them onto the base.

PAINTING THE HORSE

Horse's Coat
Base: 826 German camouflage medium brown + 846 mahogany brown + 982 cavalry brown
Highlights: raw sienna + yellow ochre oil paint
Shadows: burnt umber + Cassel earth + black oil paint

Cloth
Base: 829 amaranth red + 944 brown rose + 803 brown rose + 910 orange red
Highlights: base + 911 light orange + 835 salmon rose
Shadows: base + 814 burnt cadmium red + 818 red leather

Metal Flake Armor (White Metal)
Base: 863 gunmetal grey + 865 oily steel + 861 glossy black + one coat of diluted Tamiya smoke
Highlights: silver printers ink
Shadows: wash with black + Cassel earth oil paint + one coat of Tamiya smoke
Additional highlights were added using silver printers' ink

Metal Flake Armor (Gold Colored and decorations):
Gold printers' ink + wash using Cassel earth oil paint
Highlights: a mixture of gold and silver printers' inks

Leather Straps – Reins
Base: 826 German camouflage medium brown
Highlights: Raw sienna + yellow ochre oil paint
Shadows: Wash with black + cassel earth oil paint

Saddle
Base: 877 gold brown + 981 orange brown + 72092 brown ink + 72093 skin wash ink
Highlights: base + 911 light orange + 915 deep yellow
Shadows: Cassel earth oil paint

Shield:
Base: 926 red + 946 dark red + 980 black green
Highlights: base + 910 orange red + 851 bright orange
Shadows: Cassel earth + black oil paint

Shield Heraldry
Base: AC-51 (Andrea) golden ochre + 948 golden yellow + 858 ice yellow

A side view of the composition from farther away. The multicolored contrast of the rider and horse in comparison to the almost monochromatic groundwork makes an impressive picture.

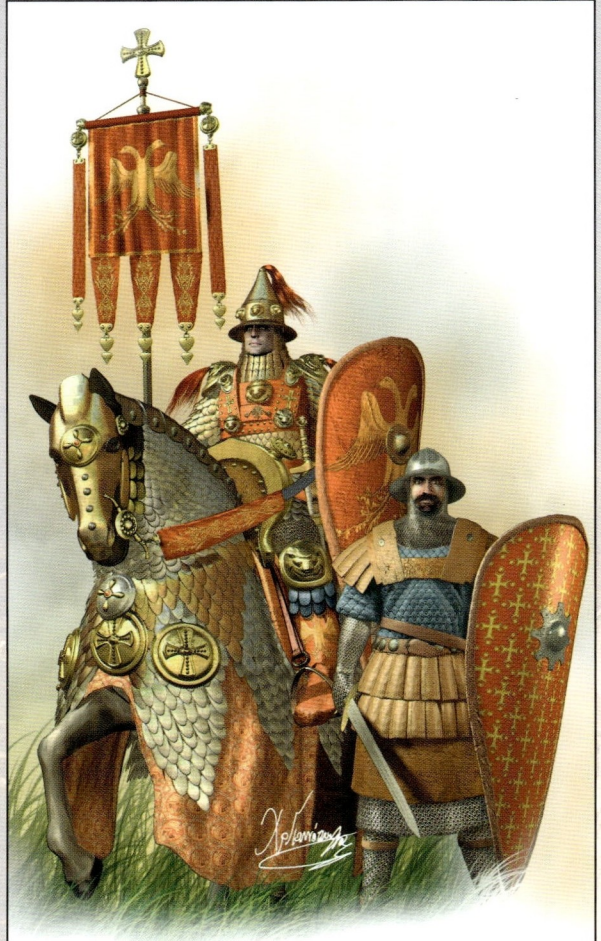

This is the "Byzantine Army" book cover that inspired Pegaso to make the figure... me also! A wonderful illustration by Christos Giannopoulos. The book is soon to be released in English!

Highlights: base + 858 ice yellow + 918 ivory
Shadows: base + 941 burnt umber + 856 ochre brown

Bow Case
Base: 926 red + 946 dark red
Highlights: base + 851 bright orange
Shadows: Cassel earth oil paint

Bow Case Decoration
Base: AC-51 (Andrea) golden ochre + 948 golden yellow + a little 996 gold
Highlights: base + 806 German yellow + 858 ice yellow
Shadows: base + 941 burnt umber

SCENERY
To make the groundwork, I first selected a dark brown wooden base measuring 7.5 x 7.5 cm from Italian firm of La Meridiana. I used natural bits of rocks, and were adjusted with the use of epoxy putty, that was textured, used a wet small stone as a stamp over the fresh putty surface

Since the two figures were not a kit set, many trials took place for the perfect fit and positioning, in order not to use a bigger surface for the presentation, despite the fact that the vignette was a 75 mm one and not a 54 mm. Distances and lengths were measured many times to ensure perfect final fitting.

PAINTING THE GROUNDWORK
Base: 950 black + 941 burnt umber + 856 ochre brown
Highlights: base + 976 buff + 918 ivory
Shadows: base + 950 black
Many washes using Cassel earth, burnt umber, raw umber oil paints

After the surface was totally dry, some small natural plants were added and fixed with PVA glue.

Positioning the figures was the next step, and this was done while wearing surgical gloves (remember, I had used oil paints, and printer' inks). The figures fitted perfectly in their corresponding pinholes. I glued them with epoxy glue, using Blue Tack as a temporarily support while waiting for the glue to set. Some small gaps were filled with putty, and after touching up with paint the job was completed.

The final job was to add the reins (made of twisted wire) to the rider's hand.

The snow was created using a Mig Productions acrylic base mixed with Microballoons and a CA glue mineral filler to enhance the sparkle effect.

This mixture was added with a brush and, while still wet, a thin layer of Microballoons was randomly sprinkled over the base. On other chosen areas, some Vallejo water-effect gel was added to represent melted snow (this became transparent when dry).

EPILOGUE
For me, this miniature was very special as it represents a period in history that both excite the imagination and the modeler's creativity. Thus, I tried to do something different, first by converting the miniature and then adding the reworked horse rather than just painting the kit as supplied. However, the feeling of satisfaction that comes in the end is also special. I hope that the detailed work process goes some way to satisfying every taste and also offers some information and inspiration.

An angled shot taken from the rear, giving a good view of the groundwork and how it rises when taking the position of the horse into account. Also note the relatively small area of the scenery.

Italian Knight
in White Armor, 1440-1450

This figure was inspired by a medieval fresco by the painter Andrea del Castagno. The fresco portrays the Florentine "Pippo Spano" (Filippo of the Scolari 1369-1426). This knight was a Count of Temesvar in the court of Sigismondo, King of Hungary.

> **90 mm**
> **Italian Knight in white armour, 1440-1450:**
> **Pegaso Models, "Elite Series" (90-039)**
> Acrylic colors: Vallejo, Andrea
> Oil paints: Winsor & Newton Artists' Series
> Metallic paints: printers' ink

PIETRO BALLONI
PHOTOGRAPHS: PEGASO STUDIO

The portrait is dated in the middle of the 15th Century. The chronological discrepancy between the personality and the armour he is depicted wearing is obvious. However, the painter chose to paint his subject wearing the more modern style of armor.

Generally speaking, the figure represents an Italian man-at-arms dressed in armor consisting entirely of plates of Florentine style armor.

The definition "white armor" is due to the effect of the near "mirror-like" finish the armor would have.

The knight wears the "Saio" or "Giornea" tunic worn over the armor which replaced the shield, which was no longer used in battle, as the method of displaying the knight's heraldry that identified the knight by name and rank.

During the middle of the 15th century, these tunics were richly decorated and often quartered with heraldic symbols or the symbol of the knights' company.

FIGURE

The figure has been cast in 19 crisp, highly detailed parts, with one part being the base. The joints are very unobtrusive, but careful attention must be paid when gluing the sword, as it must abut to the tunic at a point where there is a join. As with 99% of similar cases, it is better to paint the inside of the cloak before to gluing it on the figure. Two heads are supplied with the kit, one bare headed and extremely expressive (in fact, it is a close portrait of "Pippo Spano" taken from del Castagno's fresco) and the other wearing a rich "barbuta" helmet, a symbol of power and rank of the knight.

PAINTING

More or less half of the figure wears the "white armor." So, in this case, it will be impossible to cover the whole figure with the usual Tamiya Grey Primer Spray. If we do go down this path, we would first have to mask off all the armour parts before to spraying the primer. In fact, I chose a different solution for this figure, instead of spraying primer, I washed all the parts with soap and water, using an old toothbrush and then primed everything, using a brush, that was not armour with a light grey acrylic colour painted. My point of view is that it is very important to prime all that you possibly can as the subsequent paint will better resist the passage of time when you do. Also, you will find the paint process easier if the surfaces are clean from grease, casting residue, etc.

Next was the first problem...the Armor! A large amount of effort and concentration must go into the armour as it represents almost half the figure. The problem is, how do you reproduce the "mirror" effect on the armor plates. There are many methods and materials that can be used but still the best way to shine metal armor is using another piece of Steel. First, you have to find a piece of steel that has no sharp edges, and is very

thin. With this you can burnish the white metal until it shines like, well, steel! Make absolutely sure that the piece of steel you are using for the burnishing is round. This will prevent it from "digging-in" and damaging the surface. After the surface has been burnished sufficiently, you can use a polishing cloth to clean the surface again.

If you not been able to obtain a good steel tool, one economic substitute is the wooden toothpick... use it as a burnishing tool until it becomes black on point. Then, simply change the toothpick. The final result is good, although not as good as with the steel tool, but it will suffice.

After the whole of the armor surfaces have been cleaned and burnished, I usually give them a wash of Cassel Earth oil color. This will give the armour a "used" effect while also protecting the surface.

If I want to create an ulterior painting effect I can use pure argent (printers' ink) to paint rivets and straight lines on armor plates.

After the armor, the second main surface will be the vest. I chose an heraldic design that was in two parts, one yellow and the other blue, with a black half eagle on the yellow and half white eagle on the blue.

First step was to paint the basic colours of yellow and blue. I gave it an undercoat of medium acrylic yellow and then, on top of this I use oil colours for the highlights and shadows. The highlights were done with cadmium medium yellow, light yellow and titanium white, while the shadows were done with violet mixed with the medium yellow. I suggest using cadmium colours as they dry with a match finish.

The blue was given a dark Prussian blue (acrylic) as an undercoat, with and highlights and shadows done, as usual, with oils: azure and sky blue for the lights and black for the shadows.

The Eagle was first drawn with a pencil after the yellow and blue undercoats were dry. Be carefull to use the pencil with a very light hand so as not to ruin the paint underneath. I follow geometrical lines to draft the eagle by his main points, following its symmetry and proportions. I never try to draw the eagle's details with a pencil! For example, it is sufficient to draw the outline of the wing with the pencil, but all the feathers and details are done afterwards with the brush.

Try to think of each drawing being a sort of "kit." It can be divided into different parts and built step-by-step. The same method can be used for the damascene decorations on the cloak.

The chain mail was painted by making a wash of acrylic matt black on the metal's surface. Why use matt colour? Because, normally, chain mail was made of low quality metal. So, the chain mail has to

The belt and scabbard were then decorated to give to the knight a more "rich and powerfull" appearance.

I purposely haven't explained the painting of the face as this was done in the article about painting the Roman Naval Officer.

The most attractive part of the figure is the decoration on the cloak. A first glance, it look an awful high mountain to climb but, as I said earler, you have to start to consider this type of decoration as something to build step-by-step. Do not try to foresee the final result. Instead, divide the damascene into separate layers. First, draw the basic lines. After this, you will discover that all the decorations are no more than small designs repeated over the whole surface. All you need is suffucent patience to draw the design over the whole surface.

Remember, to realize the decorations I normally use a pencil. However, also in this case, the pencil only has to be used to realize the main points of the design.

After using the pencil, I paint the decoration with an acrylic undercoat and then use oil paints as they have the advantage of not drying on the tip of the brush. Using oils, you can paint very fine lines without aving to lift or recharge the brush.

Step-by-step, the highlights can be added, which will give a three-dimensional look to the decoration.

Normally, the textile used for rich decorations is silk. So, to reproduce a silk effect you need a satin finish, not matt.

Finally, the sword is polished metal with a wash of Cassel earth oil color and the gold metal parts were painted with printers' inks.

THE BASE

The base is very simple, just is a rock pavement with a single stair made of a different type of rock. I chose to paint the pavement in a dark rock colour and the stair in a light grey colour. Both the bases were painted with acrylics, while the shadows and highlights were done with oils. In this case, it is very useful to use a very dark color oil wash and then wipe it , using the dry brush technique for the first highlights.

I often create a texture effect by casually painting small dots with dark and light colours and then blending them with a clean dry brush, using just the tip of the brush.

appear less "shiny" than the armor Highlights on the chain mail can be done using pure chrome silver.

To create a difference between the yellow/blue of the heraldry and other details such as the scabbard, stockings and belt, I decided to paint them using a totally different color, in this case...red. The stockings were done using a cadmium red with orange highlights, the scabbard and belt were painted with a red undercoat and then orange, Naples yellow and white highlights. The result is a color between orange and pink that is completely different from the colors of the heraldry, except for the crown and the eagles beaks.

Ivan the Terrible

In the following pages, we present an amazing creation by the master sculptor, Victor Konnov, painted by Diego Ruina. The Italian master painter explains in detail the way to achieve a wonderful result, analyzing the painting techniques, and explaining the intricate design decorations.

90 mm
Ivan the Terrible: Pegaso (90-036)
Acrylic colors: Vallejo Oil paints: Winsor & Newton Primer: Tamiya gray

TEXT-PHOTOGRAPHS: DIEGO RUINA
HISTORICAL NOTES: STELIOS DEMIRAS

With regard to the size and weight of this kit, it is best to reinforce it by drilling and inserting pins, of at least 1.5 mm, to ensure the stability of the finished model. After removing any flash and eliminating any mould lines, the parts were carefully polished with a bronze wire brush followed by rubbing with a fine sponge sandpaper, working more on the wide, flat surfaces. By doing this, any mark or imperfection on the casting will disappear.

Next, I dry fitted the parts to check if any other problems might occur, while also determining what was the best working order for painting and assembly. The large, impressive cloak forces it's assembly after building and painting the figure's body. This, in turn, forces the head to be glued on last, because it has to go on after the cloak has been attached.

When decorations are highly complicated, I usually try to divide them into smaller geometrical areas and then decide the order in which these areas are to be painted. These geometrical elements can be rhomboid, squares, circles, or any other shape that have a specific gap between them.

Once all the preparation has been completed, I could move on to building the first block of the body, the hands and feet, while I glued the sleeves to the two halves of the cloak. This allowed me to attach them to the body as soon it had been painted. Two good-sized pins in the feet stabilized the model on its base, which remained extremely rigid, even after the cloak was attached.

Unfortunately, the openings of the cloak, given the size and the thinness of the parts, can easily bend, which causes a bad fit when bringing the two halves together. This can be partially covered by one sleeve and also from the fact that join corresponds to the cloak's seam. However, some putty might be needed to cover any small gap between the two parts. The partially assembled blocks were then carefully primed with Tamiya gray.

PAINTING

The peculiarity of this figure forced me to do some quick research on clothing design and decoration that might have been evident during this period. This was in order to discover the most impressive, design decoration. In the end, the best ideas for designs and decoration for the clothing styles of this period came from an old, cheap book that was in my own library.

However, what must be taken into consideration was that this model is dressed in different kinds of clothing items, influenced by different areas of Asia, and this allowed me to use many decorating styles, and even mixtures of styles, even those displaying considerable differences between them.

After determining the type of decoration designs that I would use, it was then best to sketch them a couple of times on a plain sheet of paper. This gave me a better understanding of the geometrical structure, and to decide on the primary motif, which would then be the basis for all other overlying colors.

Then, on the model itself and with a soft pencil, I drew the basic lines of this decorative motif. There is no need to draw the whole motif in detail, but only some guidelines, or reference points, which are determined using a set of dividers. For example, when painting a branch with leaves, you just need to have a line showing the start, the curve, and the end of the branch. The rest is then done directly with the brush. When the pencil preparation stage as been completed, the decoration motif is painted with the brush, taking care to totally cover all the pencil lines, and add the desired detail.

When a particular decoration is highly complicated, I usually try to divide it into smaller

The tunic is "made" from a dark blue colored silk, with a "thick" decorative flower scheme on it, while the hems are silver thread reinforced with red velvet. As a base for the tunic, I used an intense blue tone, lightened with some azure and flesh. The final result was strong and opulent enough to satisfy my expectations.

geometric blocks and determine the order in which these blocks are to be painted. These geometric elements can be, rhomboidal, straight lines, circles, or any others that have specified proportions between them. For example, using the dividers, I located the start and end points from a three centimeters length, vertical line, and then using same tool, I located the next line's start and end points, at a distance of three centimeters to the right of the first line. Then, using the pencil I drew the two lines on the model, and two small rhomboids sized in a quarter of the line, which I positioned below the center of each line. After these two semicircles, with a diameter twice the rhomboids length, were drawn, two spirals ending on the third quarter of the vertical lines on the upper half of the vertical lines were drawn and so on. The final result was a geometric skeleton sketch, onto which all the details (leaves, flowers, branches, etc,) were then painted with the brush.

In cases such as this where the geometric design is so complicated, there is always a fear of overlooking some points, or getting lost in the dense scheme. To overcome this, it is best to

Painting started, as usual, with the face. I wanted to paint a somewhat lighter skin tone, almost pale, but with particular shadowing, especially on the part that is turned to the rear. The beard is reddish, with grey ends. The cap has a fur turban, probably zibeline, a rare fur used from the time of the Huns when they invaded Asia.

partially paint the cloth. So, locate the physical subdivisions of the cloth: sleeves, front part over the belt, the rear part, two sides, below the belt, on the right and on the left. This procedure can also be accomplished by following the seams along the cloth. In this way, you can draw one section at a time, paint it, and then move to the next one.

As soon as the basic painting is done over whole area of cloth, I moved on to the highlighting, also following the partial painting method. Begin with the lighter tones of each part and when this has been done, move on to the darker ones. This method helps in following the progress in a specific sequence and also not forgetting some highlight or shadow at a particular point. There's no doubt that this is time-consuming, but it does allow you to draw extremely delicate and complicated decorative motifs, which would be almost impossible to achieve with the traditional painting style.

As usual, I began painting with the face. I wanted to paint a somewhat lighter skin tone, almost pale, but with particular shadowing, especially on the part that is turned to the rear. The beard has reddish hue, with white endings. The cap has a fur turban, probably zibeline, which is a precious fur, adopted by the Russians since the time of the Hun invasion of Asia. The cloth part is a purple color, but one can choose any desired color. I decided to decorate it with a dense dotted motif, like golden-yellow lace.

The tunic is manufactured of dark blue silk with a "thick" decorative flower scheme, and the hems trimmed with silver thread reinforced with red velvet. As a base for the tunic, I used an intense blue tone, highlighted with some azure and flesh. The final result was both intense and sumptuous enough to satisfy even my expectations. Adding the decorative motif was done initially with yellow ochre, which was later highlighted with the addition of golden yellow and white, as I moved across the folds. I then tried to recreate the characteristic, strong sheen of silk by applying many white oil paint washes on those surfaces that are more exposed to the light. These washes

Painting the cloak was really fiddly. I began by securing the two parts onto a base, in exactly the exact pose they would have when attached to the figure. I gave it a base color of red and then highlighted and shadowed in the usual manner. I then used a pencil to draw the decorative scheme and painted it with a brush using dark yellow ochre. Using yellow and white, I added the highlights, always working on just one side of the pattern.

covered the blue base as well as the decorative motif. This was repeated, although using acrylic black washes, on the shadowed areas.

For the silver bands, I first painted a gray base and then over-painted with inclined parallel brushstrokes of white, a silver wash, and then one more pass of inclined brushstrokes, as the previous ones, but this time with highly diluted black.

I chose to paint the buttons in gloss white, to obtain a high contrast with the remainder of the colors used. The boots are red, decorated with gold thread and precious stones. To paint the stones, for example a ruby, I started with a base of dark ruby red, lightened with a little scarlet red. I then placed a tiny spot of white where the light would naturally hit. I then gave the stone a coat of transparent gloss varnish. The same method was used for the other jewels, using green for the emeralds, and azure for the other precious stones. The belt was painted in green tones and then decorated with precious metals.

The painting of the cloak was really time-consuming. I began by first securing the two parts onto a base, in the exact position they would have when attached to the figure. I first painted it with a base of red, which I then highlighted and shadowed. Using a pencil, I then drew the decorative scheme and painted it with a brush using dark yellow ochre. Using yellow and white, I added highlights onto some points, always working on the same side of the pattern. Finally, I added, a very light coat of transparent gold color over the decorative motif pattern to better recreate the, brightness of the gold thread decorations. After this laborious, operation was finished, I added shadows using highly diluted black.

Next was the turn of the cloak's internal fur, also black zibeline, with bands of silver thread, like the ones on the tunic, and large gold buttons also decorated with precious stones. I then fixed the two halves of the cloak to the body. I used some putty on the rear seam line, which was then retouched with paint. I now painted the hands, necklace, and knob stick that, after painting, and along with the head, was glued into position. All that was now left was the base.

Given the figure's bright colors and the rich decorations, I felt it better to paint a light colored carpet, so as not to detract attention away from the figure.

I painted a base in a white creamy color, and decorated it in pale blue tones. I then added some more intense colors, including red, blue and green, to give more "strength" and "life" to the finished item. After attaching the figure on the base, I painted a strong shadow on the floor behind the figure. This because I imagined the figure would be in a rather dark building, in a space with low lights, and that coming from a highly placed small window.

IVAN THE TERRIBLE (1530-1584) HISTORICAL NOTES

It was on the 25th of August 1539 with thunder rumbling across the entire Russian kingdom that, despite a clear blue sky, lightning struck the Kremlin. In distant Kazan, the Tatar capital in Eastern Russia, the Khan's wife, gave her own shocking explanation of this incident. "A Czar is born among you" she announced to the Russian boyars, "He has two teeth. With the first he will devour us, and with the other, you."

This type of legend surrounded the birth of the first son to Basil III. For over 25 years, Basil III had no successor then, by his second wife, the young Lithuanian beauty Helena Glinskaya, as born Ivan the fourth. Three years after the birth, Basil became ill and died. On his deathbed, he selected seven distinguished boyars (Russian aristocrats by inheritance) to form a viceroy board, until Ivan became of age. However, in 1543, Ivan, being still just thirteen, despite all boyars' efforts to manipulate him, gathered together a group of dedicated supporters. With these supporters, Ivan, without hesitation, murdered Prince Andrei Swisky and the other boyars.

At seventeen, having officially taken the title of Czar, he was crowned in splendor as emperor. He then began to rule the country on his own, with both moderation and discretion. During this first period of his governance (1547-1560), Ivan did a superb job, reconstructing the country and the army, winning a series of wars that expanded the country's borders, cleverly and with political astuteness, reorganized church, and much else.

After conquering Kazan in 1552 and Astrakhan in 1556, Ivan increased his dominance over all areas around the River Volga. He then looked south, to the Crimea, and then west, to Livonia. He imported printing into Russia, and gave a great boost to the arts and education, attempting to make his own country into one of the most civilized and foremost in Europe.

The second period of his reign, beginning after 1560, is characterized by much cruelty, earning Ivan the sobriquet of "Terrible." Following a series of military defeats, by 1571, the Khan of Crimea was threatening Moscow. However, Ermak

Timoveyevits, who conquered Siberia, saved the situation. In February 1565, Ivan returned to Moscow with the aim of crushing for good the power of the boyars. He took for himself extended areas of land known as "Oprichnina," which translated means "personal fortune," including parts of Moscow and some of the most productive areas of the country. He continued this personal expansion until he owned almost half the country's land. He forced out the most important landholders and gave their land on the Eastern border to conscripts and "Oprichniki" (his own chosen soldiers). These mounted soldiers, who wore thick black shirts, and carried in their belt a quiver of arrows and a broom, as a sign of Ivan's decision to eliminate treachery in his country. In less than 20 years, this seizing of boyar property turned into a bloody rebellion ending with the boyars being slaughtered by the hundreds. The opposing class, members of "opritsnina", that now became landholders having seized the boyar estates, became the elite, and the country was led into a feudal regime. Near the end of his life, Ivan confessed to over 3,000 officials executions. The higher the rank, the more brutal and cruel was the punishment and eventual execution. Ivan was a man of strong passion, violent and easily irritated, even up to the point that, in a moment of madness, he killed his first-born son, Tsarevitch Ivan, by hitting him over the head with a stick. On the 18th March 1584, Ivan, by now totally insane, died. The English diplomat, Jils Fletcher, stated in his report concerning the state of Russia four years after Ivan's death, "To show the power he possessed over his liegemens' lives, Emperor Ivan Vasilievich, during his walks, if he disliked a person's face, or someone dared look at him, he would order his decapitation. This was carried out instantly and the head rolled at his feet. The general populations was in such despair, that most of the inhabitants prayed for a foreign invasion, so they could escape the heavy yoke of his tyranny."

Ivan Vasilievich, ruling as Czar Ivan the Fourth for nearly half a century, governed a continuously expanding Russia of over six million people. He was notorious as Ivan Grozny, meaning "Terrible," that revealed the terror he caused among his people. The word Czar, which means independent leader, was the Slavic equal for "Caesar." The rudeness and cruelty of his tyranny and dictatorship, cast its shadow over Russia for a long period. Of course, the Romanov dynasty that followed, whose rule was partially based on Ivan's policy, with its concentration of power and the elimination of every fire of resistance, governed Russia for over 300 years.

Finally, I applied a very light coat of transparent gold color over the decorative motif pattern, to better recreate the opulence of gold thread decoration. After this long laborious job was completed, I added shadows using highly diluted black.

Scratchbuilt Mounted Russian Knight, 14th century A.D.
Three vignettes centered on the same subject

A most original subject from Andrei Arsenyev's "Russian Vityaz" Studio, which was awarded many medals at a number of European competitions during 1998.

120 mm
Materials: Epoxy putty & white metal
Acrylic paints: Vallejo

NATALYA ALEKSEEVA & NATALYA CHARUSHINA

A stunning composition by Natalya Alekseeva and Natalya Charushina. The vignette rightly deserved the Gold Medal it won at Euromilitaire in 1998. Note how every last minute detail has been added to the base, making the whole ensemble into a masterpiece. Note also the human remains as well as the lilies, the fish in the lake, the dragonfly and the frog. Everything is so harmoniously and masterfully combined to tie in perfectly with the backdrop.

The vignette viewed from another angle. The carved inscription on the rock is clearly visible. The crow on the rock and the reeds in the foreground all serve to add realism to the scene.

A close up of the knight's face. To achieve a result like this demands many consecutive coats of careful shading.

During its early years, the fledgling Russian state had to defend itself against many enemies across all its territories. By far the greatest proportion of Russian history has been taken up by constant these bloody battles that were fought to maintain its freedom and sovereignty.

The peasants' imagination was captured by the exploits of the defenders of Russia who, in their minds, assumed mythical status. These were the Bogatyrs, who lived in the woods and marshes. The legends lived on across the generations, passed on by word of mouth.

The figure depicted here is exactly such a warrior presented in all his splendour. The scene reveals the hero at a cross-roads, contemplating the three choices carved on the rock before him: "If you proceed right you lose your horse, if you proceed left you lose your head, if you proceed straight on you loose your freedom." The human bones lying next to the inscription serve to underline the

The second vignette using the same figure but painted differently and with a slightly different base.

dangers inherent in any decision taken. Of course, the hero will choose the hardest path and proceed straight ahead to fight for freedom. The figure is, of course, a unique piece that everybody would like to see in his/her display case. The design and sculpting took over four months of full time work to complete. The skilful painting, coupled with the realistic surroundings, create an almost idyllic scene and portray the union of man and nature.

The figure was sculpted by the very talented Natalya Alekseeva and all three were painted by Natalya Charushina to create these three vignettes that recreate a part of Russian history.

THE VIGNETTE

Due to the size of the mounted figure, the base had to be of equally imposing proportions.

It was essential that the figure would be the focal point of interest and that it would unite harmoniously with the whole scene.

Construction started by gluing the rocks to the base, using two-part epoxy glue. The small bank section was made of Milliput. The horse was then placed on the base to establish its most suitable position. After trying a few different positions, the most suitable one was found and three holes were then drilled where the horse's legs would be and metal rods placed in them to act as supports. Corresponding holes for the rods were also drilled in the horse's feet.

The next step was to paint, using Vallejo acrylic paints, the lake bottom in various shades of browns and greens. A first layer of resin was then applied to the lake and left to completely dry. An alternative is to use the artificial water by Nimix or Woodland Scenics. Small plants and moss were then added with the help of diluted white glue. The second layer of resin was then applied to the lake. At this point, all the details visible through the water were added to the lake. The fish were shaped from Milliput. Note the largest one in the centre that is about to attack the dragonfly sitting on the reeds. When everything was in position, the final layer of clear resin was added to complete the lake. Pieces of expanded polystyrene were added to the bank to form the groundwork and then coated in white glue to seal them. All the plants around the lake, the lilies, the frog and the dragonfly were made of epoxy putty and they were all painted before being glued to the base, or on the surface of the lake with white glue. The skull with the rusted helmet as well as the other bones were fashioned from Milliput and painted. The trunks and the reeds were also fashioned from Milliput over a wire support. All the larger leaves were cut from thin lead sheet. The crow on the rock helps to add to the dramatic effect. The crow's body was made of Milliput with its wings being cut from Plasticard. After completing the base, attention was turned to painting the figure and its mount. The horse was painted first followed by its furnishings. The knight was the last to be tackled. As can be easily seen from the photographs, even though the basic figure is the same, it has been finished in three different ways.

The third composition has a number of different features that sets it apart and conveys the impression of an old master painting.

Viking Warrior

MIKE BLANK

54 mm
Scratch built figure

Enamel colors: Humbrol
Acrylic colors: Vallejo, Andrea
Base: Thomas Art
Epoxy putty: Magic Sculp, Duro putty
Other: printers' ink, oils.

Given the fact that I am a Scandinavian, very often I have the desire to create a Viking figure. Many of these warriors, who lived in the North, traveled immense distances, from New Land to the Byzantine Empire and till the extremes of Russia.

With this figure, I have attempted to recreate a "real" Viking, with no fancy colors, no bearskin and, of course, no horned helmet! I also wanted a figure in a different, unusual pose, such as bending forward, on a hill preparing an ambush. To achieve this, I first selected a very inclined wooden base from the Thomas Art company range.

I sculpted the figure, using a wire armature as a basis, with resin parts for the torso, hands and feet. For the head, I picked a suitable one from the Andrea Miniatures range (can someone identify which one?)

The next step was to select the desired pose. This is, by far, the most important step in creating a miniature. One has to be sure that the anatomy is correct, and to do this I refer to the relative bibliography. When the pose has been finalized, I get to "build" the naked body, using epoxy putty (Magic Sculp), using body lotion, or hand cream to make the handling easier. The tools used for the sculpting include toothpicks, with properly shaped edges, sable brushes, and a pencil-shaped simple eraser with a conical point.

As soon as the naked body was finished, I started to dress it, using thin layers of putty. I prefer to begin with the sleeves (one at a time), and then proceed to the trousers (also one leg at a time).

For the helmet, I used a resin copy of one of my own scratch built "Spangenhelm" type helmets that I sculpted some years ago.

The braided beard was created from Duro putty, and the hair was fixed in using a mixture of Duro and Magic Sculp.

Despite the fact that the figure is relatively simple and "spartan," the action pose offers an appealing and realistic result.

The greatest challenge of all while making this miniature was the shaping of the cape. I wanted to recreate one that was blowing lightly in the wind, and this demanded extra effort in the creation of the folds and creases. For the cape, I used a mixture of Duro putty and Magic Sculp, rolled out into a very thin sheet. With the use of baby powder and a small cylinder, I was able to get the impression of quite thin material. Then, very carefully, I handled the cape, and adjusted it to the figure. Only then was I able to create the creases and folds with a large flat brush. After the cape was totally cured, I added some more creases made of Magic Sculp that I shaped and refined using the sculpting tools. When all this was done, it still needed some small adjustments. These were done with a scalpel blade and some very fine Wet 'n' Dry paper.

For the belt, I used some lead sheet, while the buckle was made from Duro putty. The axe is from the Varangian Guard that I sculpted for Spain's "Elite Miniatures." The shaft was shortened and I made the hand holding it. I then added a nasal bar to the helmet from a properly shaped small piece of Plasticard and glued it to the helmet with extra strong glue. The sword is from the Viking figure that sculpted for Andrea Miniatures.

The meticulous work on the base, results in a genuine environment for the figure.

To paint the figure, I used Humbrol enamels, oil paints, acrylics (Andrea and Vallejo) and printers' inks. I really enjoyed myself while creating this miniature, as the pose is totally different from the usual "attention" pose. Maybe there is a "lesson" in all this!

The figure, just before painting. Note the different materials that we used; Duro, Magic Sculp, a mixture of the previous two, metal and resin parts previously sculpted for other figures.

The Teutonic Knights of the 13th century
The Crusaders from Germany

CHRISTOS PANAYOTOU

54 mm
Teutonic Grand Master XIII century: Pegaso (54-162)
Grand Master of the Teutonic Order XIII c.: Pegaso (54-512)
Knight Hospitaller 1250: Andrea (SM-F42)

Acrylic colours: Vallejo
Epoxy putty: Milliput, Andrea

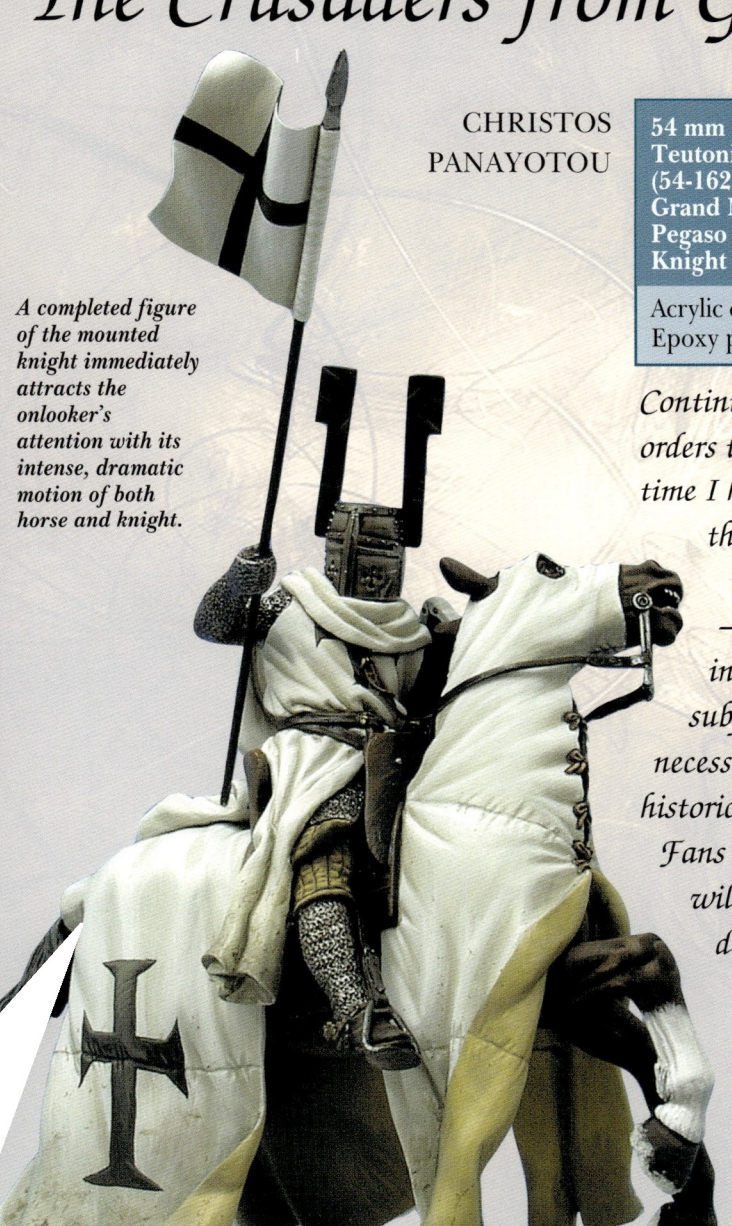

A completed figure of the mounted knight immediately attracts the onlooker's attention with its intense, dramatic motion of both horse and knight.

Continuing the presentation of the monastic orders that took part in the Crusades, this time I have chosen three representatives of the Teutonic Order — emanating from two different figure model companies — that, in my opinion, are ideal to include in an article about this specific subject, as they comprise all the necessary elements concerning both historical accuracy and number of weapons. Fans of this particular historical period will, therefore, find the following detailed presentation of great interest.

The establishment of the Teutonic Order can be traced to northern Europe in around 1130 A.D.. From 1189 to 1191, the German Brotherhood formed part of the Crusader army that fought in the Holy Land, aiding the Order of the Knights of Saint John, the Hospitallers. In 1198 – following Papal approval and blessing – the Teutonic Order acquired a structure and constitution similar to that of the Orders of the Knights Templar and of the Knights of Saint John, the only difference being that all its members should be of German origin. The Teutonic knights wore a white jupon that bore a black cross.

The members of the Order were of noble birth, while – apart from the Crusades – the Order tried to extend the Christian territories into Eastern Europe. In these endeavours, the knights of the Order used excessive violence, especially in the Baltic region and against the Slavs of north-eastern Europe. In 1235, the Teutonic Order fought the Polish Order of Dobrzyn knights that had been established in 1228. Around 1242, German-speaking populations sought and received assistance from the Teutonic knights in their struggle against the Cumans, as well as against Genghis Khan. The Order's most disastrous defeat took place in 1242, at Lake Peipus in Russia, where they fought against Alexander Nevsky of Novgorod. The most famous Grand Master of the Teutonic Order was Hermann von Salza, who was elected in 1210 and died in 1240, and was a close friend of the Emperor Frederick II.

Finally, it should be noted that the above historical narrative concerns only that particular time period in which the three figures were found, that is the 13th century. The Teutonic order still exists today.

CONSTRUCTION

Although the three figures were built and painted separately, the procedure followed was common for all of them. So, each figure, after it was cleaned of the mould and seams lines, was polished with a mini tool and primed with white primer, except for those surfaces representing metal. For all three figures, the bodies were glued together and separately painted from the rest of the parts, notably the armament, which were glued on after the painting was completed. The base colours are common for all the figures except for some details. Below are the tables showing the base mixtures of colours used on each surface.

PAINTING

Skin
Base: 845 sunny skin tone + 921 English uniform + 909 vermillion
Highlights: base + 845 + 951 white
Shadows: base + 909 + 921

White Surfaces (Jupon, Carapace)
Base: 951 white + 989 sky grey + 879 green brown
Highlights: base + 951
Shadows: base + 879 + 989 + a little 950 black

In this view, the motion of the horse can be seen to even better advantage, as well as the representation of the folds of the carapace and the figure's cape. All the crosses on the figure were very carefully hand painted with a fine brush, paying extra attention to their symmetry, as the smallest mistake would be more than obvious because of the colours used (black crosses on a white undercoat).

Cotton Clothing
Base: 877 gold brown + 941 + 845
Highlights: base + 877 + 845
Shadows: base + 941

White Areas on Shields and Helmets
Base: 951 + 989 + 844 deep sky blue
Highlights: base + 951
Shadows: base + 989 + 844

Reverse of the Shields
Base: 875 beige brown + 950 + 908 carmine
Highlights: base + 875 + 929 light brown + 845
Shadows: base + 950

This view clearly shows that all the clothing, both the knights and the horses, were dirtied along their lower areas during the painting process by adding a little black (950) and a little burnt umber (941) to the base mixture (951 + 989 + 879).

The tail was glued into position after painting the horse was completed (coat and carapace), and was painted with a mixture of black (950), grey (989) and a little Prussian blue (965). The flagstaff was replaced with one of steel rod. I had to drill through the knight's hand to secure it in place and so that it wouldn't bend later.

Horse
Base: 984 flat brown + 950 black
Highlights: base + 984 + 929 light brown + 955 flat flesh
Shadows: base + 950

Reverse of the Carapace
Base: 976 buff + 941 burnt umber + 845 sunny skin tone
Highlights: base + 976 + 845 + 951
Shadows: base + 941

Leather Parts
Base: 941 burnt umber
Highlights: base + 845 + 929 light brown + 851 deep orange
Shadows: base + 950 black

The knight's helmet, as well as all other surfaces representing metal, was first polished with a mini tool and then given two light coats of Tamiya smoke grey, while any other weathering was done with burnt umber oil paint.

The shield was painted with a mixture consisting mostly of white, a little grey (989) and a little light blue (844). Special care was taken when painting the cross, as it had to be absolutely symmetrical, while some weathering was applied to both the shield and clothes.

The imposing pose of the Andrea figure and the very unconventional helmet with the branchia offered with the kit, led us to choose this particular figure as it has also been sculpted exceptionally well.

I chose to paint the helmet in the Order's colours, using the same mixture I had already used for the shields.

The cape proved difficult to paint, as I had to paint the inner side separately before gluing it to the figure's body. After this had been done and it was secure, I painted it on the outer side.

In addition to changing the flagstaff, I also replaced the flag itself with another one made from thin aluminium foil and glued it to the flagstaff. The new flag was painted in the same colours as the rest of the fabric.

I decided not to extensively weather the Pegaso Grand Master metal parts or fabric, unlike the other two figures that were actually quite heavily weathered.

Black Parts

Base: 950 black + 989 sky grey
Highlights: base + 989
Shadows: 950

Sword Scabbards

Base: 818 red leather + 950 + 984 flat brown
Highlights: base + 845 sunny skin tone
Shadows: base + 950

The leather covering the head was designed to help the helmet fit properly and remain in place, so that it wouldn't become uncomfortable during battle.

Master of the Order was painted very carefully using the following colours: in the 1st and 4th quarters that represent the Order's cross, I used 953 flat yellow for the yellow parts, 950 black for the black ones and 951 white for the undercoat. In the 2nd and 3rd quarters, where the knight's personal coat-of-arms is represented, I painted the lions with 951 white and their red straps with 908 carmine; I also used 965 Prussian blue for the undercoat.

After the painting of the shields was complete, I shaped the groundwork on the wooden bases with epoxy putty. A little artificial snow was glued to the bases of both the mounted knight and the Andrea knight with the white helmet with the aid of white PVA glue. The remaining knight's base was painted with the following mixtures:

Ground
Base: 819 Iraqi sand + 921 English uniform + 941 burnt umber
Highlights: base + 819
Shadows: base + 921 (wash)

Stones
Base: 992 neutral grey
Highlights: base + 951 white
Shadows: base + 950 (wash)

The grass was painted with No: 80 grass green from the Humbrol enamel range and then dry-brushed with lighter tones of green. After the three figures had been glued to their bases, there then came the time for the final assembly of the small parts as well as to carry out some additional weathering on their clothes by dry-brushing them with dark brown tones.

Golden Parts
Base: 878 old gold + 950 + 941 burnt umber + 929 light brown
Highlights: base + 878
Shadows: base + 941 + 950

Silver Parts
Wash with Tamiya smoke grey.

Shield
The shield of the Pegaso figure representing the Grand

For the figure's base, I used the one supplied by the manufacturer but added some epoxy putty to make it higher. I also used carbonic soda to represent the snow, which was glued into place with white PVA glue.

Rear view of the figure, where the angle in which the shield was glued to the knight's back can be clearly seen. It is much better to glue the shield bent slightly to the left in order to attach it to the back properly.

CONCLUSION

All three figures presented in this article are excellent choices for the modeller who wants to represent knights from this particular Order among the numerous alternatives in the market. The simplicity of the colours makes assembly and painting easy for almost anyone, and I strongly advise you to choose the one you like, so that you can add a Teutonic Order knight to your personal collection. After all, detailed tables along with painting instructions, including colour mixtures, have already been presented in this article and these can be applied to any Teutonic knight figure, regardless of scale and manufacturer.

The Grand Master's left hand holding the helmet requires extra attention during the gluing process; it has to be glued in the proper position so that the helmet fits correctly as well. The only way to achieve this is to glue them together at the same time.

Viking Hersir
The Tall Warrior

90 mm
Viking hersir 8th-9th c. A.D.: Soldiers (S90-09)
Enamel colours: Humbrol

Acrylic colours: Gunze, Sangyo, Tamiya
Oil paints: Winsor & Newton
Varnishes: Humbrol
Other colours: gold typographical ink

During the dark years of the 8th and 9th centuries A.D., there were certain words that just their utterance was enough to invoke terror and panic in the hearts of the peoples of Europe and along the northern coasts of Africa. One of those words, maybe the most terrible during that period, was the one that referred to the people of Scandinavia… the Vikings!

Today, the word 'Viking' invokes a completely different set of thoughts and feelings. The picture we have today of the Vikings, much glamorised by the power of Hollywood movies, is that of tall, strong, fair-haired men who could reach any coastal or riverside country with their fast, nimble ships in order to raid, seizing anything of value they could carry.

I n my opinion, that most talented sculptor Adriano Laruccia has produced the best ever representation of a Viking with this particular 90 mm Soldiers figure. It is with much pleasure that I can pass on my experiences of painting it.

On opening the box, one can see a high quality product that guarantees a problem assembly. The parts are beautifully and crisply cast, the pose is excellent and dynamic, there is well-sculptured

PARIS TSIRCHOGLOU

This Soldiers figure has an exciting and dynamic pose. Note the oil paint highlights on the figure's hands and tunic.

Painting the shield was a long, tedious job as special masks had to be made.

The metal helmet was first polished with a soft wire brush and then Gunze Sangyo's compound was applied. The snow is simulated by the use of the excellent micro balloons.

chain mail and, of course, one of the most "wild" and "fierce" faces one is ever likely to see on a figure.

After carefully cleaning the parts, I glued together those parts that would not obstruct the painting process. As usual, I began with those parts on the figure that would retain their metal finish.

CHAIN MAIL

I started by accentuating the chain mail. First, I polished it with soft wire wool in order to clean any dull marks on the surface caused by contact to the atmosphere and any chemicals used during the casting procedure. Next, using a clean soft piece of cotton cloth, I continued polishing the mail until the cloth stopped getting dirty and the metal polish would no more. I then washed the chain mail with a mixture of 50% Tamiya or Gunze smoke and 50% liquid glass detergent. I repeated this three or four times, which is usually enough.

At this point, I think I add some additional historical, technical information concerning chain mail as I feel that some additional knowledge will help to arrive at a better scale representation. Chain mail, in regard to weather conditions, usage, age, maintenance and care, was liable to present different colours and shades of metal. A new, well-maintained chain mail belonging to a knight would have a dark metal shade with a faint blue-black tone, while one belonging to a Celt or a Viking would be rather old, worn out and very rusty. These differences can be reproduced in scale with relative oil paints washes. On this particular figure, I wanted to represent the chain mail as being worn out by used constantly in salt air, as the Vikings were without par as people of the sea. So, after washing it with smoke, another wash was applied, this time using raw umber oil paint.

Exactly the same technique was applied to the metal helmet; however, before doing so, I had applied Gunze Sangyo's compound in order to achieve the maximum possible shine on the metal helmet. For the helmet's gold decorations I used printers' ink. While this particular material might be quite expensive, it is, in my opinion, superb because of the complete absence of grain that is found in most other metallic colours.

FACE
Undercoat: Humbrol Super Enamel 93
Base oil mixture: 45% yellow ochre + 45% burnt sienna + 10% alizarin crimson
Highlights: base mixture + titanium white
Dark shadows: 60% raw umber + 40% alizarin crimson
Lips: crimson lake
Eyes: Prussian blue

After completing the chain mail, I moved on to the face and hands. The whole figure (except the chain mail, of course) was first primed with Humbrol No 1 Super Enamel. The primer was then left to dry for 24 hours, after which I painted the face and hands with Humbrol No 93, which constitutes the undercoat over which the oil paints can be applied. When No 93 was dry, I painted the face and hands with the base oil paint mixture. I then removed any excess paint from the face by vertically wiping it down using a wide, clean and absolutely thinner-dry brush. By doing this, I could remove any brush strokes by spreading the paint and, simultaneously, leaving a thin film of oil paint on the undercoat. Using this technique, quite a large amount of the oil paint base mixture remains in the recesses, while all the raised detail on the face and hands are highlighted.

These areas were then highlighted with lighter shades that were blended in with the base colour. Where a very dark tone was required, for example in the creases round the eyes and the nose, I used a very dark mixture made up of alizarin crimson and raw umber.

After the lips were painted with crimson lake, I highlighted where necessary with a mixture of crimson lake and titanium white. I painted the eyeballs with enamel matt white mixed with a little blue, while for the irises were painted in with a large circle of Prussian blue and Payne's grey. This was followed by a smaller circle of Prussian blue with a little titanium white added and, finally, in the very centre a very small dot of pure ivory black.

TUNIC
Undercoat: Humbrol Super Enamel 89
Base: Prussian blue + blue black
Highlights: base mixture + titanium white
Shadows: base mixture + blue black

Painting the figure's tunic was quite straightforward. The only contentious point I had to overcome was the tendency of the Prussian blue to dry and retain rather too much of a gloss finish, which, in my opinion, is not so realistic when painting cloth. The solution was to use the desk lamp to warm the figure and accelerate the drying time, so giving it the realistic matt finish I was seeking.

The decoration on the lower part

This photo shows the amount of work that was done to the chain mail. The wooden axe shaft can also be seen.

of the tunic and the ends of the sleeves was done exclusively with enamel colours. I used a light beige and quite a dark blue, my finest 7 Series, Windsor & Newton 000 brush and lots of patience.

TROUSERS

Undercoat: Humbrol Super Enamel 119
Base: burnt umber + yellow ochre + titanium white
Highlights: base mixture + titanium white
Shadows: base mixture with more burnt umber

CAPE

Undercoat: Humbrol Super Enamel 103
Base: burnt umber + yellow ochre + Naples yellow + titanium white
Highlights: base mixture + titanium white
Shadows: base mixture with more burnt umber

LEATHER STRAPS – SWORD SCABBARD – SHOES

Undercoat: Humbrol Super Enamel 62
Base: burnt umber + burnt sienna
Highlights: base mixture + Naples yellow
Shadows: burnt umber

After applying the undercoat, I waited for over 24 hours for it to completely and then I applied the oil paint base mixture that was wiped in the same manner as I did with the face. I then shadowed it with the burnt umber, after which I applied the highlights. For the gold decorations, I used the same printers ink that I then washed with smoke.

SHIELD

For the inside of the shield, where one can see the unpainted wood, I used, as a base colour No 110. To bring out the wood grain, I first used a mixture of No 110 + No 63 and, then, for the lighter ones, No 63, all from the Humbrol Super Enamel range.

For the designs on the face, I selected one of the many ones that can be found from a multitude of sources i.e. Osprey books or the Andrea catalogue. I also used enamel colours on the shield. The choice of the colours is obviously a matter of personal taste, as long as the colours used are those that were available during that period. In this particular case, I chose yellow and light blue. In order to get the best possible symmetry of the light blue rays, I first sprayed the yellow and then, with the aid of a glass, a new, sharp blade and Tamiya masking tape, I prepared a mask over which I carefully sprayed the light blue.

For the shield's leather strap, I followed exactly the same procedure as described above concerning the other leather straps. For the metal nails, I first painted small dots with Humbrol gunmetal and then, in the centre, even smaller dots with Humbrol silver. Finally, after the nails had completely dried, I made them look rusty with a wash of burnt sienna.

BASE

For the figure's base, I selected a Briwood Bases octagonal mount made from walnut. I wanted to represent a convincing snow-covered, simple terrain. As always, I began with the two-part Milliput putty, which was well mixed by hand. Next, in order to achieve the right representation of soil in this particular scale, I used the amazing Vallejo material into which I mixed a small quantity of sea grass, which can be seen poking through the snow.

One of the best-ever solutions for simulating scale snow is by the use of micro balloons, a kind of material used by r/c modellers. Its biggest advantage is that it does not turn yellow over time and easily assumes the desired form. The following is the technique I improvised: first I prepared a mixture of micro balloons and Humbrol satin or gloss enamel varnish. The desired density was that of thin, "runny" cream. Then, with an old brush and quick movement – because the varnish dries fast – I spread the mixture over the area where I anted the snow to be. Immediately afterwards, and before it dried, using a small palette knife I sprinkled lots of the micro balloons to make sure it would covered everything.

At this point it is worth noting that one should be very careful when using micro balloons, because it is very light and fine. For this reason, as well as the fact that the "snow" should be on the base and not in our lungs, using a mask is vital!

Finally, the final stage in representing snow in scale is to remove any excess micro balloons from the base. To achieve this, I simply blew across the base and this removed any of the material that had not adhered to the still fresh mixture.

Before closing, I would like once again to congratulate not only Soldiers, but also Adriano Laruccia for the figure's exceptional quality. It also went together easily and with absolutely no problems. Finally, I would like to express my thanks to all my good friends and fellow modellers at the "Pegaso" model club of Salonica for their invaluable assistance during the building of the figure.

The Warrior of the East
Ashigaru - Japanese foot arquebusier Azuchi momoyama period (1568-1600 A.D.)

CHRISTOS PANAYOTOU

90 mm
Ashigaru, Japanese Foot arquebusier, Azuchi-Momoyama period 1568-1600 A.D.:
Pegaso Models (90-034)

Acrylic Colors: Vallejo, Andrea (AC)

Lots of modelers, whether they are beginners or masters, are enthusiastic about eastern subjects because of the multi-colored schemes and the numerous pieces of equipment that the Eastern warriors carried. Of course, foremost of these are the Japanese Samurai, and these are also popular among Greek modelers. The Pegaso Models Ashigaru, presented here, is one of the finest – in my personal opinion, that is – figures ever released relating to the specific subject. It is for this reason that I have chosen to present it in this article.

This was the view most people would see, standing on the other side of the harquebus, as the Ashigaru were high skilled marksmen, and could achieve amazing results even by today's standards.

The Pegaso figure represents an Ashigaru with a harquebus, an early firearm. He is shown while kneeling and at the moment of aiming and about to fire. He comes from the second half of the 16th century A.D.. Ashigaru were lower-class soldiers, beneath the traditional Samurais. Japanese soldiers were part of a specific family, a kind of private army, and each with its own special emblem, the mon. These characteristics, and also the feudal system that ruled Japan, later determined the West European military system.

Harquebuses were firearms the Portuguese imported into Japan in 1543, while the country's civil war was still ongoing (1467-1568 A.D.). The Japanese improved these rifles and became such skilful shots that they were able, with a second shot, to hit the exactly the same spot as the first shot. The most famous battle in which these rifles were used was at Nagashino in 1575 A.D., when Onda Nombunanga defeated Takeda Kachioki. The family emblem, "mon" of the former warlord is the one that the Pegaso Ashigaru carries.

ASSEMBLY

The first thing that impressed me on opening the box was the sheer number of parts for the kit, especially those for constructing the armor and the ashigaru's equipment. I closely inspected each part for possible imperfections in the delicate sculpting, after which I carefully cleaned and dry fitted them to they went together well. On finding no problems, I then had to decide which parts could be glued together from the start and which should be left to paint separately. The Ashigaru is posed kneeling, ready to fire, with the rifle at his shoulder at eye level, aiming. This particular posing, and the number of the parts prevented me from assembling most of them. So, in the end, I glued just the torso (feet and thorax), and the neck protector (shikoro) to the helmet (hineno-cabuto). All other parts were fitted to a wooden block (for ease of handling while painting) and painted separately.

PAINTING

After all the parts were cleaned and glued, I moved on priming, and painting. This was done from the figure's inner areas to its outer areas. I painted all the components according to the color combinations and mixtures detailed below (all codes respond to Vallejo acrylics, unless is otherwise stated).

The very impressive figure of the finished model with all its elements is complete. The additional armor around the waist and other sensitive body area were crucial for the soldier's survival.

The rich vegetation, consisting of natural materials that are easily sourced, gives the base added realism.

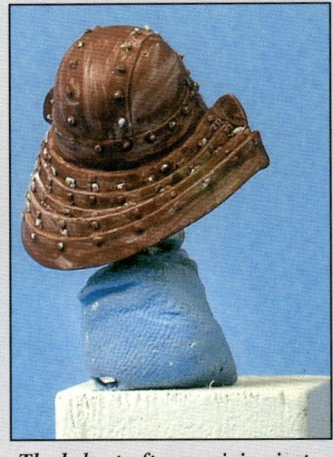

The base colors with some details have already been applied. No other part is glued onto the body, to make painting easier. Close up of foot details, including the design on the trousers, and parts of the armor.

The face was painted separately and then attached at the end, when the remainder of the figure's painting had been completed.

The helmet after receiving just one coat of the base color (926 red)

Skin
Base: 845 sunny skin tone + 860 medium flesh + bit of 909 vermillion + little 921 English uniform
Highlights: base + 845 + 951 white
Shadows: base + 909 + 921

Inner Clothing (Trousers and Sleeves)
Base: 965 Prussian blue + 966 turquoise + little 950 black
Highlights: base + little 966 + 951 white
Shadows: base + 965 + 950 black

Embroidery on Blue Cloth
Base: AC-23 violet + AC-46 crimson
Highlights: base + 951 white

Protective Cloth Over the Blue Cloth
Base: 967 olive green + 921 English uniform + 950 black
Highlights: base + 955 matt flesh
Shadows: base + 950 black

Brown Leather Parts
Base: 984 matt brown
Highlights: base + 929 light brown + 845 sunny skin tone
Shadows: base + 950 black

Black Leather Parts and Canteen
Base: 950 black + 989 black grey
Highlights: base + 989
Shadows: 950 black

Armor (Torso, Shoulders, Waist)
Base: 908 carmine red + 926 red + 950 black

Rear view of the armor. This demands careful, skilful painting and detailing in order to achieve the most realistic result.

Highlights: base + 908 + 909 vermillion
Shadows: base + 950 black

Protective Plates on Hands and Feet
Base: 908 carmine red + 965 Prussian blue
Highlights: base + 908 + 909 vermillion
Shadows: base + 965 + 950 black

Helmet
Base: 926 red
Highlights: 926 + 908 carmine red + 909 vermillion
Shadows: base + 950 black + 965 Prussian blue

Violet Parts of Armor
Base: AC-23 violet
Highlights: base + 951 white
Shadows: base + 950 black

Right view of the figure, with items of armor covering almost the entire body, especially the knuckles. Look at the figure's accessories, including the leather case and canteen, the latter being made from a pumpkin painted with black lacquer.

The level of sculpting on all the parts was superb, with the highest accolade going to the armor plates, that very realistically follow the supposed movement of the figure.

Close up of the flag, adorned with the Onda family's emblem (mon), mounted on a bamboo flagstaff. Painting is much more difficult than it might appear, and needs a lot of attention in order to attach it correctly

White Cords on Armor
Base: 989 sky grey
Highlights: 951 white

Feet Bandages
Base: 970 deep green
Highlights: base + 953 matt yellow + 955 matt flesh
Shadows: base + 950 black

Socks - Waist Overcloth
Base: 951 white + 884 stone grey
Highlights: base + 951
Shadows: base + 884 + 950

Sandals - Ropes
Base: 914 green ochre + 921 English uniform + 941 burnt umber
Highlights: base + 951 white
Shadows: 941 burnt umber

Large and Small Swords
Base for scabbard: 950 black + 989 sky grey
Highlights: base + 989
Shadows: 950

Base for handle: 875 beige brown + 950 + 908
Highlights: base + 955 matt flesh + 951 white
Shadows: base + 950 black

Leather Case
Base: 875 beige brown + 926 red + 950 black
Highlights: base + 955 matt flesh
Shadows: base + 950 black

Flag
Base: 908 carmine red
Highlights: 908 + 909 + 851 deep orange
Shadows: base + 950 black

Detail of the harquebus with the painted wood grain, adding both realism and the appearance of real wood.

Rear view of the figure, showing the flag and the second pair of sandals hanging from the waist. Also seen are the details on the Katana sword scabbard, where flowers and other decorations accentuate the black lacquer paint. Note the figure's waist area, and the flag mount, also the flagstaff and armor parts representing lacquered surfaces. These have been given a coat of satin varnish.

The correct recreation of the facial expression is always important when painting a face, as it must combine with the figure's pose. The face of the aiming ashigaru, special care is needed in the area of the eyes so that they show how the warrior is concentrating on his target.

Close up of the helmet and the neck protector strips. Below the helmet can be seen the mounting point for the flag, that needs a very secure bond because of the weight of the flag.

Flag Staff (Bamboo)

Base: 976 buff + 941 burnt umber + little matt flesh
Highlights: base + 951 white
Shadows: base + 941

Harquebus (Wooden Parts)

Base: 875 beige brown + 929 light brown + 908 carmine + 950 black
Highlights: base + 929 + 955 matt flesh
Shadows: base + 984 matt brown

Gold Parts

Base: 878 old gold + AC-27 gloss black + 941 burnt umber
Highlights: base + 878 + bit of 953 matt yellow
Shadows: base + gloss black + 941

Silver Parts

Base: 865 oily steel + AC-27 gloss black
Highlights: 865
Shadows: base + gloss black

After completing the painting of all the parts, I then painted the details, including the embroidery, small designs, and also the Onda family emblem (mon) on the flag. Those parts of the armor that would have been highly lacquered received a coat of satin varnish, to get them a somewhat glossy appearance. Final assembly was carried out after the base was made and painted.

THE BASE

After I had completed the painting of most of the figure, it was attached with glue to the base that I had build with epoxy putty. While the putty was still dry, I positioned small pebbles and "tree stumps" (tree branches or roots) onto it. After the putty had hardened, I attached the static grass and the rest of the vegetation with white glue,

When everything was dry, I painted the ground with 873 field drab, the stones with 989 sky grey, and the grass with Humbrol's No 80 grass green. After these colors had also dried, I used washes of burnt umber oil paint and, then when this was also dry, I dry brushed the base colors with lighter tones. Building and painting the base took me a week's work, and the figure took six weeks. The final assembly took three days, starting from the bottom up, and waiting after each operation for the glue to set. Then, finally, after two months of pretty intense work, just a few spots of touching up completed the job.

EPILOGUE

Despite the fact that this Pegaso Models figure is both time consuming and hard work, the result will more than satisfy you. Because of its level of difficulty, I would not recommend it for the beginner, while fans of this era will definitely choose one of the market's finest pieces to add to their collection.

Step by Step

"THE LOST DOCUMENTS"
How to sculpt 75 mm figures for comercial casting

SCULPTOR: MARKUS ECKMANN
PAINTER: JÜRGEN NIRSCHL
TEXT ARRANGEMENTS AND
PHOTOGRAPHS' CAPTIONS:
COSTAS RODOPOULOS

SCULPTING

I was very pleased when I was asked to sculpt a woodland warrior for Sparta-Modellbau, because I generally love the theme of Indians. This theme includes the chance to create scenes enbeded in the nature and I really enjoy it to create such scenes. Inspired by a painting of Robert Griffing, I began to sculpt an Indian warrior finding some documents of the white people in the deep forrest. When I showed the completed figure in our home forum, Jürgen

MARKUS ECKMANN

I was born on the 16th of November of 1968 in Ingolstadt. I am married since 1998 with my dear wife Nicole. We have two children, Sebastian and Anna.

I am a proffessional sculptor and I sculpt for several companies, but also for private collectors and when there is a little bit time left – for myself.

I love it to create small scenes and mostly I try to tell a little story....

I have no preferd theme or time in sculpting figures, because I think every time has his own likeness. I also love it to be a moderator in two Web boards (HZ-Forum, HistoricusForma) and to write articles for figure journals, because I enjoy the excchange of knowledge....and the friends I found because of this works.

Upper and right view. The base construction has incorporated many hours of careful painting and many kinds of natural vegetation to have this realistic result.

Front and upper vie. Notice the matching of the figure colors with the environmental surrounding. This kind of binding is also crucial for the most completed picture of the scene.

A ground level shot, with the front of the Woodland Indian, showeing all the different elements that need to be painted, with careful definitions.

Nirschl offered me to paint this figure for me and I was really honoured about this. Then we had the idea to add a second figure to this scene and when I told Sparta about this idea, they wanted to have the second figure as a comercial figure, too. The idea was not to add a second Indian but a American settler. I like it to show different ethnics in one scene...because there is no need to show only war and fights. We know, that there always have been friends between the White Men and Indians... The vignette shows a settler and his indian friend on the trial...perhaps they are on the hunt. Then they find a box of ducoments in the forrest and the indian is very intersted on the written words...

Step by Step

The settler's figure finished and placed on the vigniette base.

The Indian's figure, painted in vivid colors.

Painting the different elements, of the indian figure.

Patience and programmed painting is needed to enhance every detail of the sculpture, on this beautiful figure.

Figures

To sculpt the figures I used the same way as always. First I created the armature and the the figure growes step by step. For me, sculpting is mostly a progress of development and so the figure has always the chance to communicate with me...

I think there is no need to decribe the whole process, because I think the pictures tell their own story, much more detailed, than a text can describe a sculpting course. We will present in photographical order the making of the American settler, as for space purposes is not possible to present both of the figures.

Base

I wanted to surround the figures in a soft and silent scene in the deep forrest. The rocks have been sculpted in a very easy way. First I glued some Polystyrol-plates together, to get the height I wanted to have. This plates are used to isolate houses and you can buy it in every hard ware store. After glueing he plates I carved the basic shapes out of them. The next step was to cover them with a thin layer of Magic Sculp. To engrave them I have used real stones and some old silver foil. The next was the old and broken tree. I used a piece of wood and broke it into two parts. The part I most liked, became the base for the tree. The tree was coverd with a thin layer of putty and then I engraved the structure of a bark. The next step was to add some roots and some broken boughs. Finally I added some mosses to the rocks and the tree. To create the mosses was very simple. I just put some points of Magic Sculp and engraved them with a short cuted brush.

The finished vigniette from a different ancle, showing the standing Settler and the left part of the indian

The back side of the vigniette from a right ancle. Note that the base construction and detailing is all around and not only in the front place.

JURGEN NIRSCHL

My name is Jürgen Nirschl and I am a figure painter since 1996. My first paintjob, a German Tanker (Verlinden, 120mm) was also the beginning of being a part of the "KIT-Figurenjournal," the leading Journal here in Germany. In the following years I earnt some honours as a master-painter in USA, Italy and Germany.

Since the Figure Competition "Duke of Bavaria" started I was a member of the organisation team. I take the photos of the winning figures for the beamer-presentation after the show.

PAINTING
Figures

Both figures are sculpted excellent and they are surrounded with lots of filigree details, like the books, the weapons and so on. The casting of the figures is superb and so I had not much work to do before I was able to start.

The figures have been primed with the airbrush and as always I have used Humbrol White. After two days I began with the first basic layers of color (I use acrylic colours for painting). I saw a lot of pictures showing Indians in white or cream coloured shirts, but I wanted to paint with much more contrasts.

For the basic layer I have used a mix of carmin, Violett and a little bit Black. For the shadows I added a little bit black and for the highlights I added a little bit Tint Flesh.

For the trousers I used a blueish tone of Vallejo, wich harmonized very well with the shirt. The settler shirt was painted with a mix of Andreas Confederate grey and the jacket was painted with a dark brown of Vallejo. I added a little bit Prussian blue to the basic mix to shade the folds od the jacket. It took me some time to create the sight of a old and very often used leather, because it is very hard to paint this realistic. The trousers have been painted in a dark ochre. The highlights are mixed with a little bit of flesh. I always paint by instict and eye, so there are no exact proportions, on color mixes, you must just do your trials and search for the best results.

Base

The base was very well sculpted and prepared by Markus but I had a lot of possibilities to let it grow. When we found the perfect position for the both figures, I fixed the footprints with a little bit of Magic Sculp. Then I added some more roots to the base and painted them. I finished the tree with lots of drybrushing. I used different tones of brown, green, ochre, and yellow . I used the same way to paint the rocks and the vegetation. I have used colors of Andrea and Vallejo, in many different mixes and variations, that makes it impossible to describe, as i am sure you will find your way, depending on the chromatic result you expect to have. Finally I added some moss powder, which is used at the railway modelling and it worked very well to get the whole scene much more realistic tied. Finally the figures have been added to the base and the work was finished. This common work took me several weeks, but every week was worth it and I enjoyed every minute working on it.

Step by Step

SCULPTING THE TRAPPER

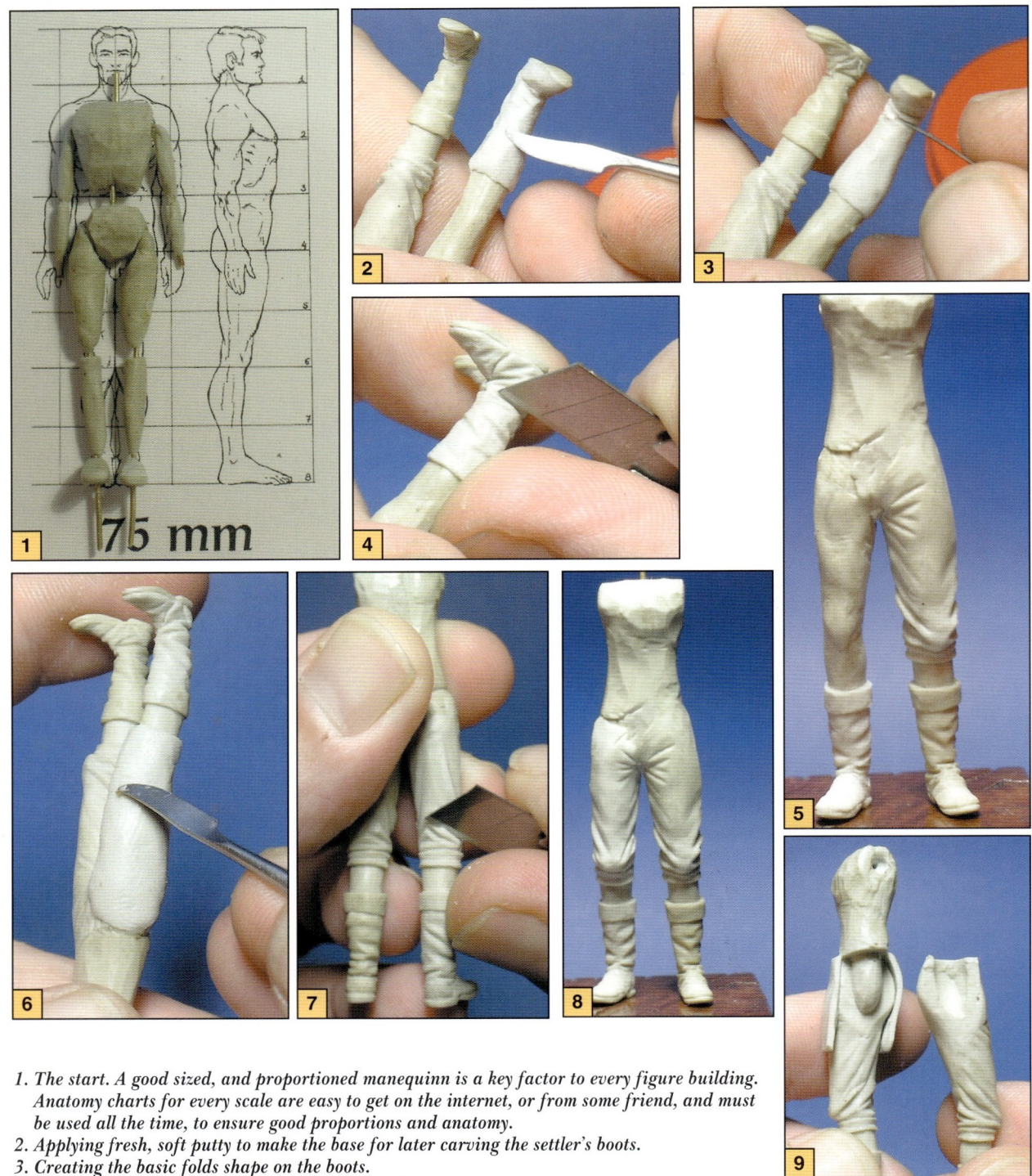

1. The start. A good sized, and proportioned manequinn is a key factor to every figure building. Anatomy charts for every scale are easy to get on the internet, or from some friend, and must be used all the time, to ensure good proportions and anatomy.
2. Applying fresh, soft putty to make the base for later carving the settler's boots.
3. Creating the basic folds shape on the boots.
4. Carving the boots in more detail and ginig final shape to the folds.
5. One leg is ready, the other is on the basic fleshing stage, waiting the trouser clothing and detailing carving.
6. Layering the base putty "blob" that will be formed in a trouser part, and will be carved accordingly when this will be dry.
7. Sculpting folds and creases on the trousers.
8. Both legs are ready and the symmetry is a crucial factor, to check before deciding to stop sculpting these parts.
9. Checking the left leg placement on the rest of the body sculpture, to ensure perfect fit.

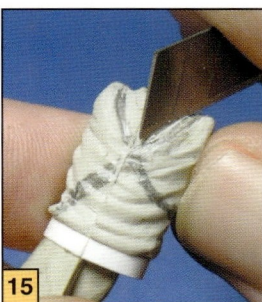
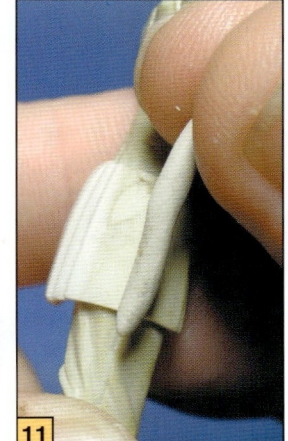
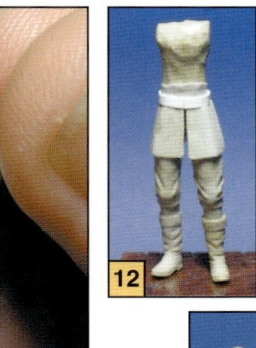
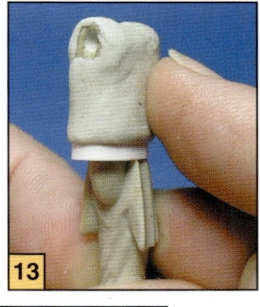
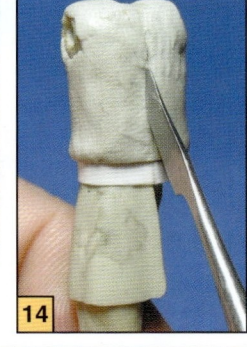
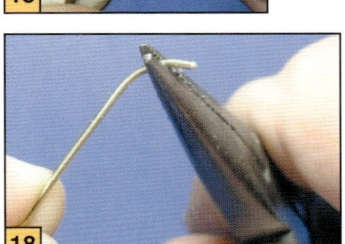

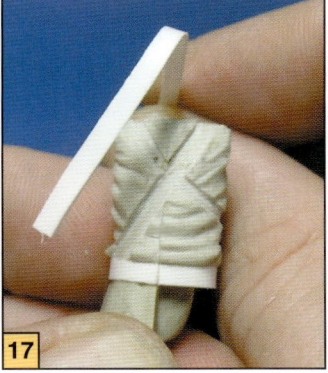
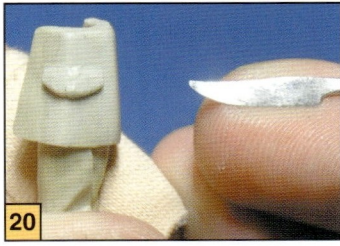
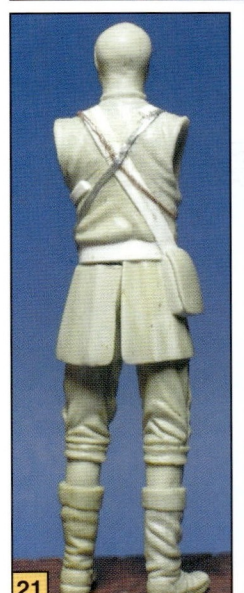

10. Carving out the putty layer to make the desired shape on the waist area.
11. A fresh putty "snake" ready to be used on the desired part of the figure. Further formation and smoothing will follow, before drying and carving the desired shapes.
12. Using a bended plasticard stripe for the waist belt.
13. Layering the putty on the torso for making the jacket. The layer must be of the same thickness, all over the body.
14. Modelling the putty layer with the right tool, makes work easier and faster.
15. After marking it with a pencil, starting to curve the belt's path on the cloth body.
16. The recess, for the belt placing is now ready.
17. Uisng plasticard stripes for making the wide belts of the figure. This way, the width is always the same and the shape sharp, with no triming needs, as if we would make this out of putty.
18. Preparing a paper clip piece for the hand armature.
19. Using a blade to curve the different lines of the figures main body clothing.
20. Using a carving tool to clean out the forms and finalise the shape of the figure parts.
21. A serious part of the job is already done. We have the pose and the main body shaping, and the detail additions start to take their place on the figure.
22. Note the clean definition of the arm insertion area, as well as the sculpture of the figure's side area.

Step by Step

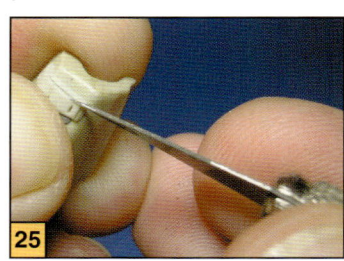
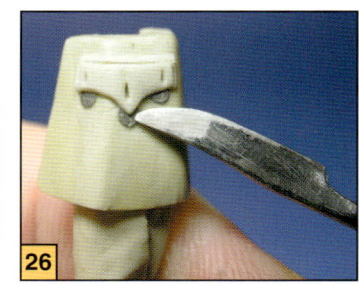
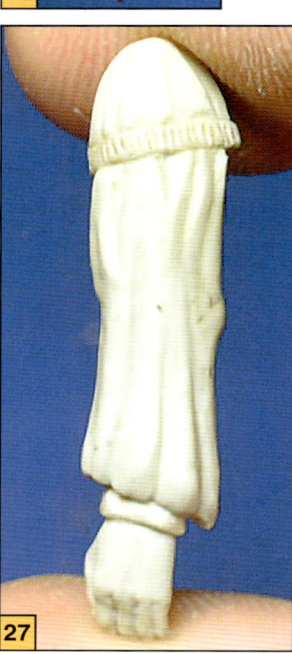
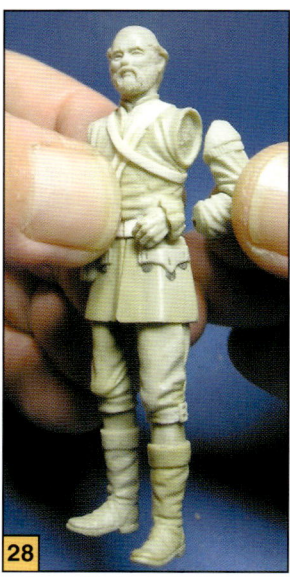

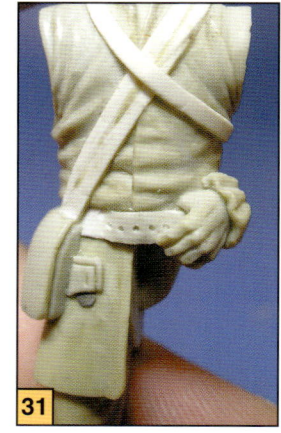

23. Part of the armature is now sculpted as the upper arm, while the lower part awaits its turn!
24. Making the cloth folds more intense with the modelling knife.
25. Cleaning the definition seams of the pocket.
26. Positioning and detailing of the buttons with the appropriate tool.
27. A finished arm as a separate piece. The fit on the body is checked many times, so there will be no problem in assembly after the casting of figure in white metal.
28. Checking the arm in its final position, while the rest of the area of the body is already sculpted and dried.. Refining and trimming with sand paper is always needed to have the perfect match.
29. Close up on the left part of the body. Clever "cutting" of the figure parts is needed, for easier casting and assembly of the figure kit. Check the arm positioning spot.
30. Test fit of the hat on the head. If more trimming is needed, now is the time to do it!
31. Check the grab of the hand on the waist belt of our sculpture.
32. The easy way to make buttons. Punching a lead sheet with a hard wire piece, against a rubber piece.
33. Placing the buttons in the front part of the jacket, with the help of a modelling knife.

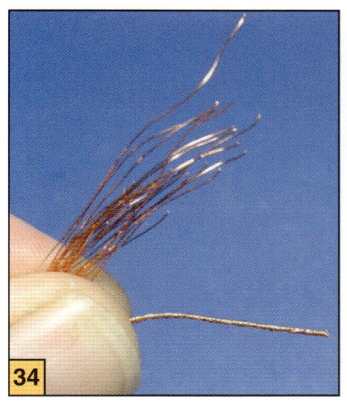
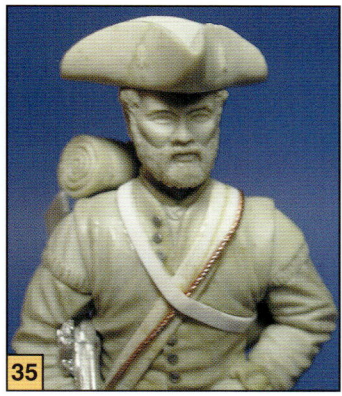
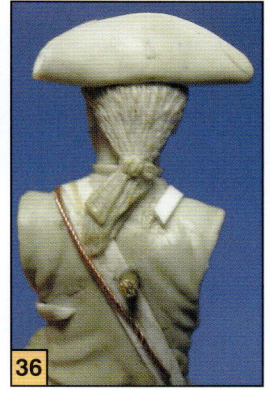

34. Different gauge of wire is very handy to have in the working bench. By twisting it you can make different kinds of ropes. By using it to punch lead foil you can make detail items, such as buttons.
35. Repeating trials, is time consuming, but is the only way to assure that every element of the figure will fit perfectly when time comes to finalise it. Everything must look physically matched and not just "left" there.
36. We always check equally both sides of the figure, for securing perfection in all details. Note the realistic flow of the hair on the back .
37. Many trials of the hat, are needed, before we decide that we have a perfect fit, on a physical position on the head.
38. It's really important, to take attention on the symmetrical sculpting of the eyes, and distances from the nose.
39. Note the fine sculpting of facial hair and the clearly defined details on the upper part of the body.
40. Close up, in the area of the chest and waist. Plenty of details, that will make the difference when the figure is properly painted. 75 mm is a scale that allows, the sculptor plenty of space to superdetail the figure.

133

Step by Step

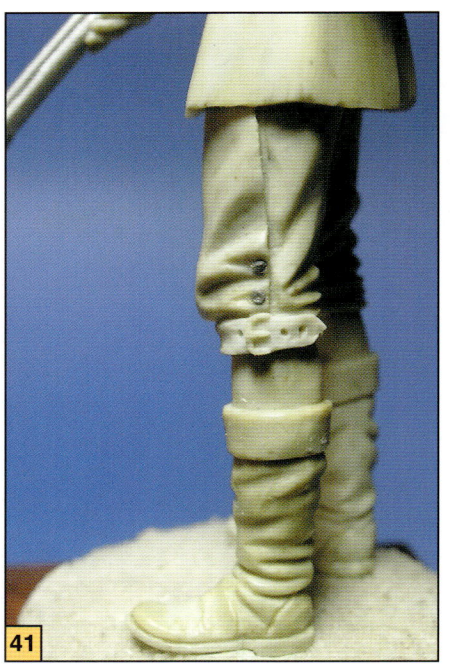

41. Lower part of the leg. All details must be clean and defined, so the painter will have to do the minimum effort to make them stand out. Nice creases on the boots are an interesting touch always.
42. The front side of the figure. You can see the detail and proportions of the finished piece.
43. The finished figure has the distinctive look of the specific era.
44. The back side of the figure. Check the clean final areas of the figure that will end in a smooth casting, and a figure with no much to clean.
45. Note how all the different parts of the figure match up harmonically on the finished piece. Well defined creases and folds always make, more interesting the figure and painter's life much more easier.

INDIAN

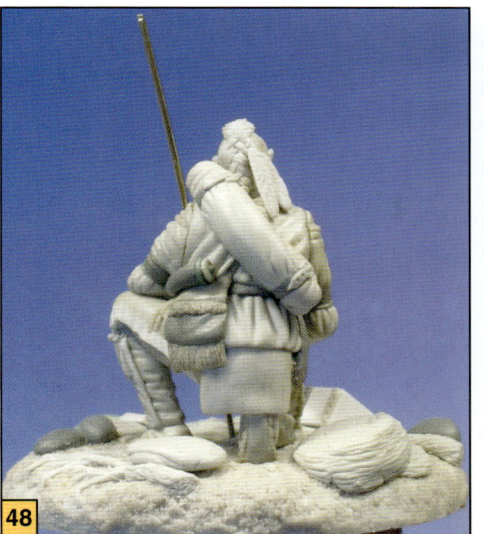

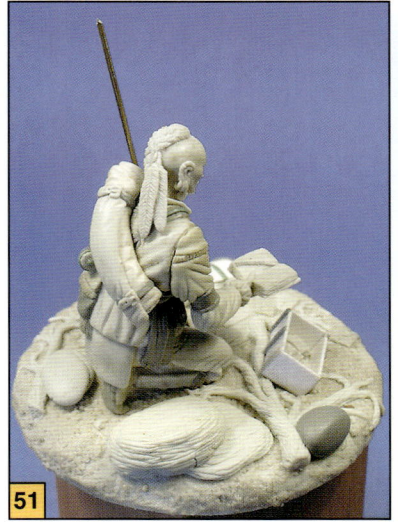

46. The front view of the finished figure, unprimed, revealing the different materials used for the composition.
47. The right side of the figure. Clean sculpting is a key for good production and easy painting.
48. The back view of the figure. Note the detailed work on the indian's bag and the rest of his equipment.
49. The left side of the figure, showing, the fold work of the sculptor as well as the detailed accessories, that have been matched on him.
50. The detailing on the front part of the figure is evident, as well as the elaborate base, showing roots, rocks and the human accessories that catch the Indian's attention.
51. The back right side of the Indian's figure. See the tight fit of all the figure's parts and accessories, that are needed to show a realistic result.
52. The finished Indian. A beautiful sculpture in a nice pose and offering many pocibilities for a vignette composition.

Step by Step

GROUND WORK AND VEGETATION

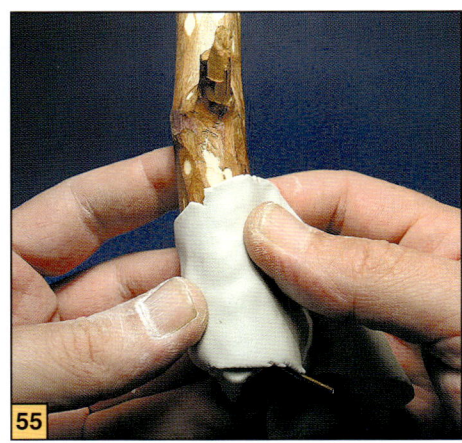
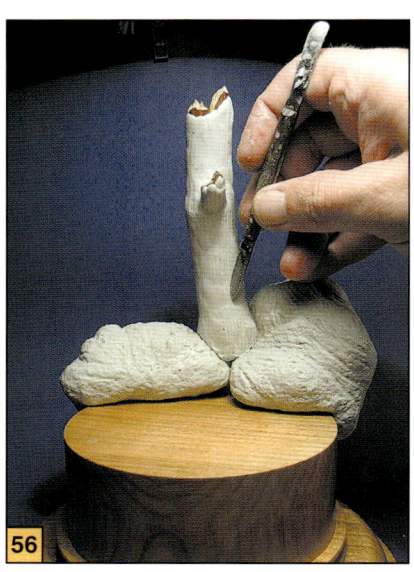
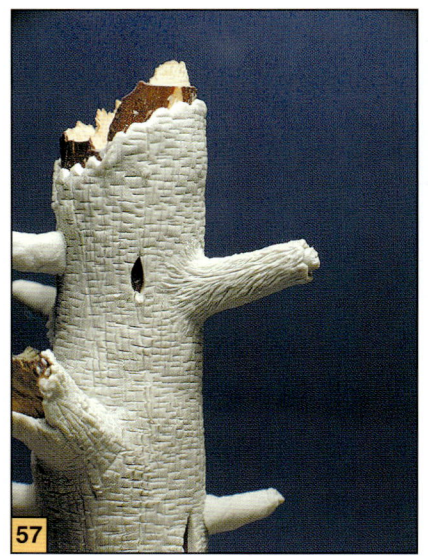

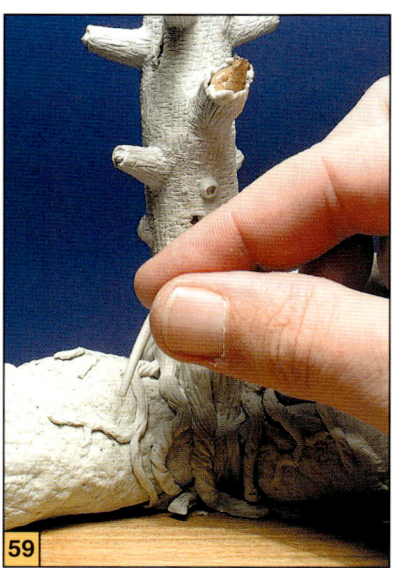
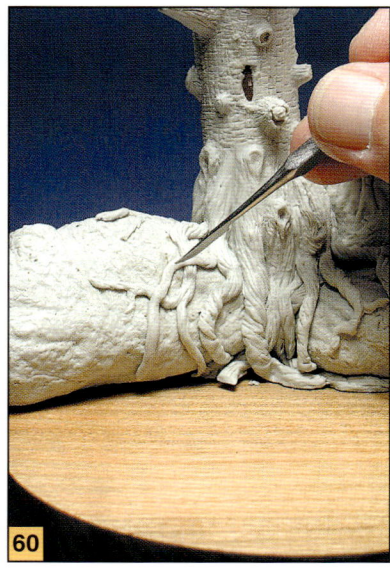

53. Testing a piece of wood, as the tree trunk, between the rocks.
54. The rocks with their securing pins ready to be placed, on the base.
55. Layering fresh putty on the wooden branch. We must apply it in an even sheet, before its ready to be textured.
56. Sculpting carefully the surface of the tree trunk. Realism is essential and reference material will prove a treasure.
57. The sculpting on the tree bark is almost done, offering a view of the tree skin.
58. Modelling the details of the tree makes it more and more realistic. It is really important, that before this work you have studied, pictures of the "real thing."
59. Adding putty "snakes" that will create the tree roots, after they will be formed and sculpted.
60. Carefully modelling the texturing of the external tree roots. Elements like this, add realism and atmosphere to the groundwork effort.

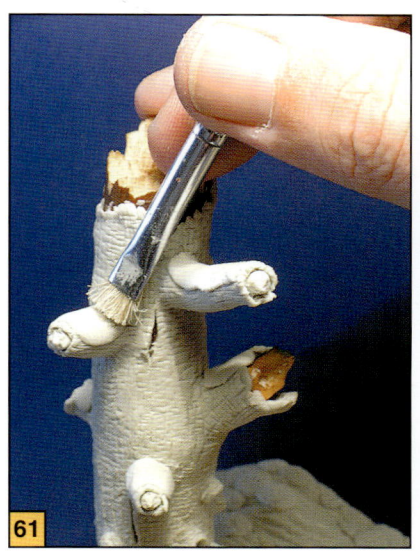

61. Using a hard brush to create the moss effect over fresh layered putty.
62. The rocks, and tree complex placed on the vignette base.
63. Close up on the sculpted tree. Check the detailed sculpting that took many hours, but will repay when painted!
64. The finished tree, with lots of moss on the bark and the surrounding area.
65. The long grass, that will be used , as one of the kinds of vegetation. Can be found either in railroad supply shops, or eeven from an old brushes hair!
66. The long grass is taking place with some white glue.
67. The sea weed - grass is already placed on the ground.
68. Getting a small portion of sea weed that will be adjusted on the base with some white glue.
69. The groundwork is more or less finished, and waiting the painting stage.

Step by Step
MAKING THE ROCKS

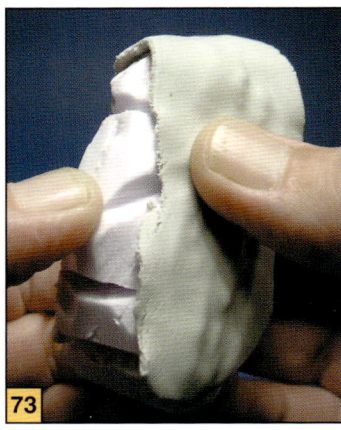

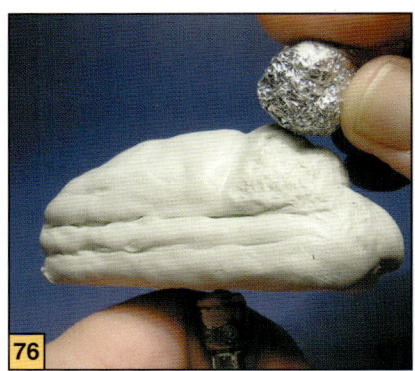

70. Using pieces of insulation sheets, for the main body of our rocks and ground formations, has the advantage of light weight, low cost, and easy manipulation.
71. With a sharp knife we can give the shapes we like to these pieces and mainly pre - form the rocks.
72. Preparing the putty, flattening it, before applying to the base material.
73. Layering a putty sheet over the insulating material. It must be evenly covered, because this will make sculpting easier.
74. Forming the rock surface, with the appropriate tool.
75. Texturaizing with a natural stone with intense surface characteristics.
76. Texturizing with a simple ball of aluminium foil.
77. The rock is texturized in a very realistic way, with many marks that will be enhanced during painting and make the compilation more attractive.
78. Checking many different combinations, before finalising the setup, will give us the more possible options to decide the best scheme for our vignette.
79. The rocks covered with putty and textured. Notice the bottom of the parts that will have a perfect match to the wooden base, since we have performed the fit many times before.

Scottish Officer of 42nd Regiment
Officer of Black Watch

Figure: Pegaso Models (54-214)
Base: Andrea Scenery (AS-009)
Acrylic colors: Vallejo

Uniforms of the Napoleonic period are among the most attractive for figure modellers as well as for the end viewer. Most miniature manufacturers offer either a small or wide range of figures from this period, representing most of the fighting nations. Among the more spectacular subjects are the Scots, because of the characteristic kilts they wore… and still do! The tartan designs on the kilts differ between the regiments, with probably the most famous being the 42nd Regiment of Foot, The Black Watch. The release by Pegaso of an officer of the 42nd Royal Scots' Regiment immediately caught my eye and I was motivated to paint, especially the kilt's tartan. The procedure I followed is described below step-by-step.

CHRISTOS PANAYOTOU

The 42nd Royal Regiment is among the older, more famous and historical regiments of the British Army. It is known as the "Black Watch" because of the dark colors of its tartan.

The regiment was raised in 1739, after the unification of many independent units of the British Army. The Regiment took part in many campaigns, including the USA, Canada, and also in Cuba and India. It took part in a number of important actions during the Napoleonic Wars. In 1801, during the battle in Alexandria, members of the regiment captured the standard of Napoleon's " Invincible Legion ". I saw action on many of the Napoleonic Wars' battlefields, including Quatre Bras and Waterloo.

Jacket (blue)
Base: 965 Prussian blue + 950
Highlights: Base + 965 + 951 white
Shadows: Base + 950

Black Parts (feather – scabbard)
Base: 950 + 965 + 989 sky grey
Highlights: Base + 965 + 989
Shadows: Base 950

White Parts (socks, belts, gloves)
Base: 951 white + 989 sky grey + 921
Highlights: 951
Shadows: base + 921 + 989 + 950

ASSEMBLY

As with every figure kit, I began by cleaning off the flash from all 10 parts included in the kit. This was done with the modelling knife, and then followed up with sanding with fine sandpaper to give each part a perfect surface. I then polished all the parts with a fine wire brush in the motor tool, and carefully drilled a 1mm hole into each foot and inserted a length of paper clip to secure the figure to its base.

Then I dry fitted all the parts before deciding which parts could be glued at the beginning and which could be left and painted separately. I then secured them to individual wood blocks for easier handling. The final operation before beginning the painting proper was to spray them with white color primer. After this had completely dried, I started painting.

PAINTING
Flesh
Base: 845 sunny skin tone + 909 vermillion + 921 English Uniform
Highlights: base + 845 + 815 basic skin tone
Shadows: base + 909 + 921

Jacket (red)
Base: 908 red + 984 matt brown
Highlights: base + 909 + 953 matt yellow + 845
Shadows: base + 926 red + 950 black

Step 1

Step 2

Step 3

Cloth Girdle

Base: 926 red + 965 Prussian blue
Highlights: Base + 909 + 845
Shadows: Base + 965 + 950

Gold Thread

Base: 996 gold + 953 yellow + 929 light brown + 984 brown
Highlights: Base + 996 + 953 + 951
Shadows: Base + 929 + 984

Brass

Base: 878 old gold + 984 + gloss black
Highlights: 878
Shadows: Base + 984 gloss black

TARTAN (KILT – CAPE)

Painting the tartan was divided into 6 steps so as to achieve a realistic recreation. I should also point out that there are many different military tartans, and each regiment has its own specific design. So, after checking the reference for what was required in this instance for the 42nd Regiment, I painted it in the following sequence:

Step 1

Painting the kilt and cape in the base color, which should be a little darker tan the actual tartan color and act as an under layer. The mixture used for this was 965 Prussian blue + 950 black in 70% – 30% proportion.

Step 2

Next, I painted the green stripes (vertical and horizontal, leaving even spaces between them, so the dark undercoat would show

An overall view of the Andrea Miniatures figure, with the resin scenery and wooden base I used to get a complete presentation, that is recreated in the first instance, by the regiment's formal uniform.

Step 4   Step 5   Step 6

through). These stripes are a mixture of the under coat with 967 olive green added, as, in reality, also the blue fibres cross with the green ones.

Step 3

At this point, I painted, using 967, the blocks that form on the cross sections of the dark green stripes. Note, at this stage, there are squares of blue, dark green and green color on the cloth.

Step 4

Using 950 black and a really fine brush, I painted a very fine line on the edge of each other wide strip, either horizontal or vertical. After this every block will have a black outline.

Step 5

Using black and a fine brush again, I painted a thin line through the center of each green square. These lines cross each other in the center of the green blocks.

Step 6

On each stripe (horizontal or vertical) that includes blue and dark green squares, I paint in each alternate one, two black lines leaving the intermediate blank, onto which I then paint four thin black lines.

Using this process, you can paint any tartan, but, of course, you must first check the reference for each colour combination, according to the specific regiment you are interested in.

A view of the cape that was really carefully painted before attaching it to the figure. It was painted with the same 42nd Regiment tartan design that I painted the kilt.

After all the figure parts were painted, I assembled them using two-parts epoxy glue. The complete figure was then attached to its resin scenery base, that is a recreation of a stone floor with a small part of a wall and railing.

BASE

The base kit is from the Andrea Miniatures range and was painted in acrylics as described below:

Bricks
Base: 908 red + 984 brown
Highlights: base + 845 sunny skin tone
Shadows: base + 950 black

Wall (beige parts)
Base: 977 desert yellow + 984 + 917 beige
Highlights: base + 977 + 917 + 951 white
Shadows: base + 984 + 950

Wall (grey parts)
Base: 989 sky grey + 950
Highlights: base + 989
Shadows: base + 950

Stone Road
Base: 990 light grey + 950 + 921 English uniform
Highlights: base + 990 + 951
Shadows: base + 950

The left hand holding the sabretache had to be glued on and be painted before assembling it to the body, otherwise it would be impossible to attach it correctly later.

EPILOGUE

I hope that this article will help in some small way to show you how you go about painting tartans. The most important thing is to fully understand the lines of the tartan's design. To do this, you need correct and "clear" reference material, and then to plan it on paper before proceeding to paint it. Scottish soldiers are an appealing subject for miniature painters and the fact that they wear tartan plaid should not discourage us but, on the contrary, motivate us to try our skills o obtain the best possible result.

Pirate Madagascar 1720

This bust is the second in a row that I have painted and I must say it was really worth every minute of my free time. To be honest, at first I was a little afraid of assembling and painting busts because of their large surfaces. However, I now believe that if one invests a little time, the result can be amazing.

CHRISTOS KATSELOS

150 mm
Pirate, Madagascar 1720: Latorre Models (BU/02)
Acrylic colours: Vallejo Printers' inks Printers' oil paint

Using highly diluted colours helps the modeller avoid any undesirable brush strokes. This photo shows that the highlights were gradually brought to prominence; this is the most difficult thing to achieve when painting medium size figures

The kit consists of six parts, two of them being the metal earrings, for those modellers who have a traditionalist's view of what a pirate should look like. Apart from the earrings, the rest of the parts are resin of excellent detail and quality and almost without any mould lines. The assembly process took hardly any time and it all went together without any problems, with almost no filler required.

washed all the parts with soapy water using an old toothbrush. I then drilled a hole in the underside of the bust, glued in a pin (snipped from a large paper-clip) and secured the bust to a wooden base. As the bust is cast from resin, it is quite light and easily handled during the painting procedure without fear of an accident. The remainder of the parts were also attached to other temporary wooden bases and given a coat of Gunze primer.

PAINTING

On this occasion, I did not apply a primer coat on the main part of the bust, but instead applied four quite thin coats of the base color, using Vallejo acrylics (Model Color). In order to attain the desired result, I had to make a mixture made from many different colors. As far as colors are concerned, I really like to experiment quite a lot, especially when getting a skin tone, until I get the shade I am looking for. In this particular case, I wanted to represent a weather-beaten type of skin due to its long exposure to the sun and sea, also maybe a little sweaty. To do this, I used several shades of brown and red, thus beginning with a somewhat dark base.

Base: brown sand + red beige + English uniform + flat brown + magenta + sunny skin tone + vermillion

After the base color had fully dried, I began the highlighting procedure. I separated the skin surface into two main areas: one up to the neck and the other one from the neck up. With an area of skin this large, I wanted to focus on each part separately. The first highlights were done by adding different

Each hair of the feather was painted separately, as I wanted to avoid dry brushing. Look closely at the weathering and the dusting on the hat.

amounts of red beige to the base colour for 5 – 6 tones. I then used sunny skin tone for another 5 – 6 tones and, finally, basic skin tone for the final ones.

I always use colors that are as diluted as possible and continuously remove any excess paint from the brush before applying it to the figure. To make the shadows, I gradually used burnt cadmium red, magenta, purple and, finally, a touch of black. Where I wanted to give the skin an unshaven (5 o'clock shadow) appearance, I applied a coat of highly diluted black and burnt umber oil paints. I painted the eyeballs flesh + silver grey, while for the pupil I used black + Prussian blue, which was then highlighted with sky grey.

Right from the start, I wanted to give the face a rosy skin tone, to reflect the pirate's long exposure to the sun and sea.

Belt

The leather belt was painted with a mixture of English uniform + flat brown + mahogany brown. It was then highlighted with English uniform, tan yellow and flesh, especially on the most worn areas. The shadows were done after adding flat brown and black to the base mixture. The badge was painted with a base mixture of English uniform + chocolate brown + black + old gold. For the final highlights and shadows, I used oil paints and printers' inks:
Highlights: burnt umber + gold, gold, gold + silver
Shadows: burnt umber, burnt umber + black.

Neckerchief

For the neckerchief I chose a brown-yellow colour.
Base: orange brown + golden brown + yellow
Highlights: golden brown + yellow
Shadows: orange brown + purple

For the white line I used English uniform + medium grey + off-white
Highlights: medium grey + off-white
Shadows: English uniform

Hat

The hat requires a lot of work, as it covers almost the 50% of the whole surface of the bust. To paint it, I used black, brown and blue tones.
Base: black + English uniform + Prussian blue
Highlights: base + violet
Shadows: base + black

For the weathering and the dust I used various tones, including English uniform, tan yellow, U.S. field drab, flesh and sunny skin tone. One could also use various pigments because, with this size of hat, they will also help with the painting and weathering procedure.

Ribbon

Base: vermillion + red + brown beige + Prussian blue + black
Highlights: base + vermillion + light orange + sunny skin tone
Shadows: base + brown beige + Prussian blue + black

The feather was painted in several shades of medium grey and white, and then, afterwards, I used brown and yellow filters in order to relieve the monotony.

The painting procedure was a really pleasant task; I can highly recommend this bust to any figure modeller who is able to appreciate its excellent detail and quality and is also willing to devote some time in order to make it into an outstanding exhibition item.

19th Century Bersaglieri Officer
The Italian army's "fighting cocks"

The reason for choosing this particular Pegaso figure is the uniqueness of the subject, certainly as far as the 19th century is concerned. The Italian bersaglieri is a subject far removed from the usual English or French ones – at least for us – although they do hold a special place in the history of the Italian army, mainly because of the many actions in which they have taken part right up until today.

CHRISTOS PANAYOTOU

The Bersaglieri corps was founded in 1833 and, from the outset they constituted an elite unit of the Sardinian army and, later, the Italian one. Their characteristic blue uniforms, as are presented in this article, remained the same until WWI. They used to wear the black slouch hat with the rooster's feathers (the trade mark of the bersaglieri corps) both in war and peace. Finally, it is worthy of note, that during the Crimean war they also wore a red fez with a blue bobble.

54 mm
Bersaglieri Officer: Pegaso (54-136)
Acrylic colours: Vallejo, Andrea

PAINTING

The painting process began – as usual – with the cleaning of the figure, removing the mould lines, etc., and then burnishing it with a motor tool. Next, I assembled those parts that would not get in the way of painting, i.e. the left hand with the sword scabbard and the leather pouch on the front of the belt. The figure parts were primed with a spray primer and then left to dry for 24 hours before starting to paint. I used the following color mixtures:

Flesh
Base: 845 sunny skin tone + 921 English uniform + 909 vermillion
Highlights: base + 845 + 951 white
Shadows: base + 921 + 909

Uniform
Base: 965 Prussian blue + 950 black
Highlights: base + 965 + 951 white
Shadows: base + 950

Blanket
Base: 950 black + 965 Prussian blue + 989 sky grey
Highlights: base + 965 + 989
Shadows: base + 950 black

The Pegaso bersaglieri is an ideal basis for experimentation with blue shades, mainly because of the many different blue surfaces on the figure.

The distinctive broad stripe on the trousers required a little more attention when being painted, to ensure that the correct shade, as well as the appropriate highlight shades were obtained.

Rear view of the figure, where all the piping can be seen, as well as the characteristic rooster feathers on the bersagliero's hat.

Gold Parts
Base: 996 gold, followed by a wash with smoke grey + Tamiya clear yellow

Silver Parts
Base: 865 oily steel
Highlights: base + 997 silver
Shadows: base + 950 black

BASE (GROUNDWORK)
Base: 929 light brown
Highlights: base + 953 matt yellow + 951 white
Shadows: base + 941 + 984 wash

The grass was painted with a rather dark green and, when dry, dry brushed with lighter shades of green.

After I had finished painting all the parts, they were glued together and the whole figure then positioned on its base.

CONCLUSION
The Pegaso Bersaglieri is an excellent figure that presents no problems to speak of, which makes it ideal even for beginners. Because of its overall quality, it will surely reward anyone who buys it as a collector's item, the end result often being far better than expected.

The excellent sculpting of the whole figure, particularly the small details, such as the epaulets, made the painting of the gold piping that much easier, as it easy for me to highlight even the knots on the fringe.

Sash
Base: 844 deep sky blue + 965 Prussian blue
Highlights: base + 844 + 951 white
Shadows: base + 965 + 950

Sleeve Turbacks
Base: AC-46 crimson + 965
Highlights: base + AC-46 + 951 white
Shadows: base + 965

Black Parts (Hat and Accessories)
Base: 950 black + 921 English uniform + 989 sky grey
Highlights: base + 989 + 921
Shadows: 950

Feathers
Base: 970 deep green + 950
Highlights: base + 970 + 845 sunny skin tone
Shadows: 950 + 970 wash

White Parts
Base: 951 white + 989 sky grey
Highlights: base + 951
Shadows: base + 989 + 950

Gold Threads
Base: 953 matt yellow + 996 gold + 941 burnt umber + 984 matt brown
Highlights: base + 953 + 996
Shadows: base + 941 + 984 wash

Chasseur of the Imperial Guard
The Emperor's Bodyguards

CHRISTOS PANAYOTOU

Mounted cavalrymen of the Napoleonic Wars have always attracted the attention of modellers because of the variety and diversity of their uniform colors and the equipment they carried, especially the troopers and officers of the Chasseurs a Cheval de la Garde Imperiale, who wore their own version of the colorful hussar uniform. Their primary mission was to guard the Emperor: they were, in fact, his personal guard.

54 mm
Figure conversion
Horse - Mounted Superior Officer, Polish Guard Lancers 1810: Metal Modeles (COFPOL)
Figure - Mounted Hussar 7th Regiment 1808: Metal Modeles (C7H)
Historex: accessories

Acrylic colors: Vallejo, Andrea
Epoxy putty: Andrea Sculp

As already stated, the Regiment of the Chasseurs a Cheval de la Garde Imperiale was charged with the protection of the Emperor Napoleon, both on the battlefield and elsewhere, as its primary duty. The Regiment was established by decree of 1804 and consisted of four cavalry squadrons. Each squadron was made up of two platoons and was responsible for the security of the Emperor while in his residence. On the battlefield, a brigadier and four privates accompanied him at all times as a close, personal guard.

Concerning the type of uniform the Guard Chasseurs wore at Waterloo, information is somewhat ambiguous, as they might have worn the hussar uniform without the distinctive red pelisse, or the other, green uniform with tailed coat, the surtout. However, it appears that uniforms of all types

The spectator's attention is attracted by the beautiful Chasseurs a Cheval de la Garde Imperiale green shabraque with yellow braid edging, these being very prominent. In particular, the yellow braiding should be painted in such a way so they give the impression that they are actually yellow wool, both the broad line around the saddlecloth and the eagles at the corners. For the yellow braiding, the color I used was matt yellow 953 to which I added a little orange brown 981, very little red brown AC-18 (by Andrea), with pure yellow and white for the highlights.

were worn during that great battle. In May 1815, the commander-in-chief of the Guard Chasseurs raised a contingent of 1,267 troopers. During the battle they were forced to give ground under the powerful frontal charge and flank assaults from two British brigades.

CONSTRUCTION

Having wanted for quite some time to build (and paint, of course!) a mounted Guard Chasseur and there being was no 54 mm kit of such a figure on the market, I decided to make one. So, after researching the market to find out if there was a figure I could use as a basis, I selected two mounted figures by Metal Modeles, the Polish lancer officer and the hussar trooper, as well as a Historex chasseur. From the Polish officer kit, I used just the horse while, from the hussar one, just the figure; from the Historex kit I used just some necessary equipment.

Before starting the construction, I made some drawings of the changes that needed to be made to the figures so that they would accurately represent the chasseur I had in mind. Drawings such as these should be made before any complicated, time-consuming building and painting procedure, and should describe all the stages in detail. In this particular case, the building procedure was divided into two main parts: one for the horse and the other for the figure. I selected the Polish officer's horse because it was not so different from the one used by a chasseur. The necessary conversions concerned the careful removal, using a new blade, of all the relief symbols and other details of the Polish harness, as well as removing the inner, thin line of gold braid around the edge of the shabraque. After the removal of all the detail that was applicable to the Polish officer, the surface of the shabraque was carefully given a coat of filler, so that any marks left from the earlier procedure was removed. When the filler was completely dry, it was gently rubbed down until it was smooth. Finally, I also removed some of the harness ornamentation that was applicable to an officer's horse furniture. After all these conversions had been completed, I put the horse aside and focused on the figure.

As mentioned, I planned to use the Metal Modeles' hussar as a basis for my chasseur. This required the conversion of just the hat and the right arm, as well replacing the sword and sabretache. I used the head from the hussar kit, although the shako worn by this one was not correct as the chasseurs wore a fur colback. So, after removing all the cords and the peak, etc. from the original hat, the whole surface given a thin coat of epoxy putty, which was then scribed with a needle to give it the distinctive fur texture of the chasseur's headgear. While the putty was still wet, I attached the characteristic plume, also taken from the hussar kit, to the top left side. The red cloth bag hanging down the

For the horse I used the one from the Metal Modeles mounted Polish lancer officer, which in my opinion, is one of the best horses on the market. To paint it, I used the following mixture: red leather 818, burnt umber 941 as the basic one, with orange brown 981 for the highlights and burnt umber 941 for the shadows. This photo shows the detail on the Chasseurs a Cheval de la Garde Imperiale sabretache. For this, I used one from the hussar kit by Metal Modeles. After removing the existing designs I replaced it with the chasseurs Imperial coat of arms insignia made by Historex. Great attention is required during the painting procedure, due to the small area and the numerous colors involved, whereas the shabraque mixture was used for the yellow braid.

right side of the colback was made of putty, whereas the raquettes were a Historex part. As far as the hands were concerned, I used the complete left arm from the hussar kit, while the right one was converted to the desired position. So, to complete the conversion, I cut the right arm at the wrist and elbow and, after gluing them in the desired position, I filled the gaps with epoxy putty. At this point, it should be pointed out that, when converting a figure, always cut the parts you want to change at the respective joints, i.e. the knees, the waist, the neck, etc. Then, when the parts are glued back into the desired position, cover the gaps with putty, following the figure's anatomy. The above were the only major conversions concerning the figure, although some minor ones were also made; I had to change the sword and sabretache. From the hussar sabretache, I removed the regimental number and the bay leaf wreath surrounding it and replaced them with the Imperial coat of arms insignia used by the Guard Chasseurs. This, and also the chasseur sabre and scabbard, was also sourced from Historex. Before proceeding with the next step, the painting, I attached the harness to the horse and prepared the figure, except for the pelisse, the sword and sabretache.

Almost the entire surface of the red pelisse (typical hussar dress) is shown here. The red used is carmine red 908, whereas the highlights were done with sunny skin tone 845 and the shadows with red 926. The fur was painted black, with the most difficult part of the pelisse, the braiding, was painted yellow just like the other yellow parts of the figure and saddle.

PAINTING

The painting procedure began with the horse. After it was given a coat of primer, the following color mixtures were used:

Horse
Base: 818 red leather + 941 burnt umber + 950 black + a little 981 orange brown
Highlights: base + 818 + 981 (in 4 – 5 tones)
Shadows: base + 950 (in 2 -3 tones)

Shabraque
The shabraque was chasseur green with yellow braiding; it also carries two yellow eagles, one on each side, while all the leather harness straps were black. Officers usually sported a leopardskin shabraque.

Chasseur Green
Base: 970 deep green + 875 beige brown + 950 black
Highlights: base + 970 + 955 matt flesh
Shadows: base + 950

Yellow Braiding
Base: 953 matt yellow + Andrea No: 18 red brown
Highlights: base + 953 + 858 ice yellow
Shadows: base + Andrea No: 18 red brown

Leather Harness Straps
Base: 950 black + 951 white + 965 Prussian blue
Highlights: base + 951 + 965
Shadows: 950 black

The main parts of the figure's body were painted during the assembly process, except the sword and sabretache. The major differences between the uniforms of the troopers and that of the officers was, the latter's plume was white instead

The base plays an important role in the presentation of a figure. For the Chasseurs a Cheval de la Garde Imperiale trooper I decided to create a snow-covered setting that would contrast with the dark horse.

of the red over green for the troopers. The fur of the officer's pelisse was white, while the troopers' were black. In addition, the trooper's braiding was yellow wool and that for an officer was gold bullion. The officers' waist sash was gold thread with green slides, while the troopers' was green with red slides. It is also worthy of note that officers did not carry a cavalry carbine or the twin shoulder belts (one for the cartridge pouch and the other carrying the carbine swivel). An officer carried a single shoulder belt of black leather trimmed along the edges with gold bullion and a sabre.

Skin Tone
Base: 955 matt flesh + 909 vermillion + 981 orange brown + 921 English uniform
Highlights: base + 955 + 951 white (in 4 – 5 tones)
Shadows: base + 909 + 921 (in 2 – 3 tones)

Hat (Colback)
Base: 950 black + 879 green brown
Highlights: base + 879
Shadows: 950 black

The figure's green and yellow surfaces were painted in the same way as the harness.

Breeches
Base: 976 buff + 981 orange brown + 941 burnt umber
Highlights: base + 951 white
Shadows: base + 981 + 941

Pelisse
Base: 908 carmine red
Highlights: 908 + 845 sunny skin tone
Shadows: 908 + 926 red

The lining of the pelisse was painted white, while the fur was painted in the same way as the colback.

Gold Parts
Base: 878 + old gold + Andrea gloss black
Highlights: 878 + 996 gold

Silver Parts
Base: 997 silver + gloss black
Highlights: 997 silver

In this photo, one can see the light beige breeches (made of deerskin) of the Chasseurs a Cheval de la Garde Imperiale, a color that is difficult to replicate correctly. In order to obtain it, a number of mixtures must be made. I used the following colors: buff 976, very little sunny skin tone 845, very little orange brown 981, very little burnt umber 941 and very little flat yellow 953, adding white for the highlights and burnt umber for the shadows, and keeping a soft tone throughout.

After the painting was complete, all the separate items were glued into place and the figure fixed to its base. I also simulated some melting snow on the ground.

CONCLUSION

The trooper of Chasseurs a Cheval de la Garde Imperiale really grabs the spectators eye with its diversity of colors, so I also decided to make an officer. However, that said, the regiment of Chasseurs a Cheval de la Garde Imperiale are not recommended for beginners or intermediate level figure modellers, only to the more experienced ones, because of the amount of detail on the uniforms, as well as the difficult assembly process. It should not be forgotten, that conversions such as this particular figure are very difficult, even for the experienced modeller. Apart from that, the subject is really impressive when finished and worth the effort.

BIBLIOGRAPHY

1. Philip Haythornthwaite, Uniforms of Waterloo, London: Blandford Press, 1974.
2. Information and details from Historex.

Louisiana Tigers

The countless cinema productions concerning the American Civil War have led us to identify the uniforms of the opponents according to their color: blue for the North and grey for the South. But, during the war, many strange uniforms appeared, the most unusual being that of the Zouaves.

> **54 mm**
> **Corporal Louisiana Tigers: Elite (RG/54.09)**
> Acrylic colors: Vallejo
> Oil paints: Winsor & Newton
> Epoxy putty: A+B
> Grass: Heki

PANAYOTIS TSETSEKAS

The Louisiana Tigers was perhaps the most famous Zouave unit of the American Civil War, the creation of the lawyer and mercenary, Roberdeau Wheat. In a comparatively short time, the Tigers proved to be one of the most famous battalions in the Southern army, their main attributes being their unrivalled courage, toughness and striped breeches. They took part in the battles of the First Battle of Bull Run, the Jackson Valley campaign and in the Battle of Gaines Mill, where Wheat was killed. Without their major, the Tigers ceased being a reliable unit and, in the end, the remainder of the Zouaves were scattered among other battalions of the Confederation.

PAINTING

Raul Garcia Latorre has sculpted the Elite figure, which represents a sergeant of this particular battalion as he was during the First Battle of Bull Run in 1861. It is distinguished for its faultless pose and incomparable quality of its fine detail. The sergeant wears the usual blue jacket of the French Zouaves with the red patches and the striped breeches that were the unit's well-known feature. It is worth noting that the breeches were made from mattress material, which resulted in the great variety concerning the size and number of stripes. The assembly of the figure presented no great difficulties and I could quickly move on to the painting.

Painting techniques when using acrylic colors are much different from those for enamels or oil paints. Instead of the usual blending, the highlights and shadings are done with washes, over the dried base color, of lighter or darker shades of the same base color, but highly diluted with water. This process should be followed for as many times as it takes to attain a successful result. For the highlights, I usually use 20 to 25 lighter shades, while for the shadows just 7 or 8 darker ones. Below is a table showing the colors used, as well as some comments on the individual parts.

Hands - Face

Base: matt flesh 955 + vermillion 909 + orange brown 981 + magenta 945 + burnt umber 941
First highlights: base + 955 matt flesh
Final highlights: 951 white
Shadows: base + 909 + 945 + 941
Final shadows (oil paints): mars brown + brown madder alizarin + purple madder alizarin. The use of oil paints for the dark areas of the face and hands gives greater depth and more vividness.

Jacket

Base: Prussian blue 965 + black 950 + turquoise 966 + green grey 886
First highlights: base + 886 + grey blue 943

An overall view of the figure. Note the shadows on the blue jacket.

Final highlights: 886 + beige 917
Shadows: base + black

Red Patches
Base: red 947 + a little black green 980
Highlights: base + light orange 911 + sunny skin tone 845
(Repeat this also for the beret)

Breeches – Socks White
Base: 951 white + gold brown 877 + orange brown 981 + black 950 + English uniform 921 + stone grey 884
Highlights: 951 white
Shadows: 877 + 981 + 950 + 991

Blue Stripes
Base: US blue grey 904 + pastel blue 901 + grey blue 943 + very little 965
Highlights: white
Shadows: 965 + very little black

Gaiters
To paint the gaiters, it is recommended to use the same mixture as that used for painting the breeches, but replacing the stone grey 884 with 885 pastel green in order to obtain a different shade of white.

Leather (belts, bag, etc.)
Base: black + very little 981 and bright orange 851
Highlights: 981 + 851
Shadows: black

Rear view of the Tiger. The flask was painted with Vallejo metallic colors.

Painting the stripes demanded an enormous amount of time. However, the end result justifies the efforts of the modeller.

After completing the highlights and shadows, the leather parts were given one or two coats of satin varnish to give them a much more realistic appearance.

Gold Parts
Base: flat yellow 953 + gold 996 + brass 801 + golden yellow 948 + olive green 967
Highlights: 953 + 996
Shadows: wash with 941 + 981

All the above acrylic colors are from the Vallejo range, while the oil paints are from Windsor & Newton. The base was built from A+B epoxy putty, which was then shaped with toothpicks. The vegetation – a mixture of paintbrush bristles, Heki grass and dried plants – was painted in green and yellow shades. Finally, placing a wooden log on the base completed the groundwork.

CONCLUSION
This Elite figure gives us the opportunity to paint one of the most outlandish and complicated uniforms to appear during the American Civil War. Without doubt, no one with an interest in this particular conflict should be without this figure in his/her collection. Even if this is not your particular period of history, this figure will give you hours of enjoyment.

The correct representation of the face is the key to a successful appearance.

Step by Step

FRENCH CUIRASSIER 1812-1815
The "Heavy Armor" of the French Army

The wide variety of uniforms and colors from the Napoleonic period is a constant challenge for the enthusiast to choose the most impressive among them.

> **90 mm**
> **Mounted French Cuirassier: Andrea (S8-F34)**
> Acrylic colors: Vallejo, Andrea
> Oil Paints: Winsor & Newton
> Epoxy putty: Andrea Sculp

CHRISTOS PANAYOTOU

A mounted figure in 90 mm is always very impressive.

One of the more popular organizations are the French Cuirassiers, due to the combination of large metal and clothed surfaces, and the added challenge of painting horses.

The French cuirassiers were a major part of Napoleon's heavy cavalry arm of the French Army. They took an active part in the majority of the campaigns and were present at some of the major actions during the war.

Many figure manufacturing companies have fed the constant demand for figures, both mounted and on foot, from these specific regiments. So, in consequence, Cuirassiers can be found, mounted or on foot, in almost every scale. For this article, I have used an Andrea Miniatures of Spain kit of a mounted Cuirassier in 90 mm scale.

The mounted cuirassiers, founded in 1803, were one of the foremost symbols of the French cavalry during the Napoleonic wars. Famed for their courage and élan against the squares of the British Army. At Waterloo, the heavy French Cavalry, especially the cuirassiers, spearheaded the French cavalry's assaults, led by Marshal Ney, against the British squares although they failed to break them. At Waterloo, twelve regiments of cuirassiers were present, each consisting of almost 960 men. The regiment differed from each other by their individual facing colors on the collars, cuffs and turnbacks.

In 1811, the cuirassiers, in an effort to rationalize their helmets, were issued with new ones. However, by doing so, it seems the authorities also tried to economize as well and the new headgear was much inferior in all ways to the earlier ones. In fact, many of the "old hands" retained their old ones, as these were much stronger, offering better protection. On campaign, the distinctive red plume, mounted on the left side of the helmet, was detached and stored. The hose hair manes were black for troopers and NCOs and white for trumpeters who, incidentally, also wore a different colored uniform (usually the reverse of the remainder of the regiment).

The horses' harness and shabraques were identical for NCOs and troopers of all regiments (only the regimental numbers, embroidered on the rear corners of the shabraque and on the ends of the valise mounted behind the saddle, were different). Cuirassiers carried the cavalry carbine, Type Mosqueton M9, hanging from a belt on his right hand side, as well as a bayonet. They also carried the straight 120 cm long heavy cavalry sword. The cuirass could withstand sword blows or a bayonet thrust, but not a bullet, while the weight of it severely hampered the riders movements, especially if they became unhorsed, making them "sitting ducks, " as happened regularly during the Battle of Waterloo.

ASSEMBLY

As with every mounted figure, and especially the larger scale ones, this Andrea kit, consists of many parts (52). These make up into the rider and his horse. There is also a photo-etched sheet containing the regimental numbers but I did not use these. In the mounted cuirassier's large box is also found four pages of instructions, including all the details for preparation and assembly.

I decided to begin the assembly with the rider after cleaning all the relative parts and polishing them with the motor tool. I concentrated on the surfaces that represented metal, specifically the helmet and cuirass, and burnished them to a high shine. Before final assembly, I first dry fitted the parts to check for any possible problems, such as gaps that would need filler and the correct sequence for gluing. After all this was done, I decided I needed to break down the trooper's painting procedure into sub assemblies:

1) Head with helmet, onto which I attached all the parts at the beginning, except the mane.
2) Cuirass and arms.
3) Feet, with boots and stirrups.
4) Trooper's equipment, these were painted separately and attached to the figure after all the painting was completed.

All the different parts, in the four phases of assembly and painting, were primed with white spray, except, of course, those surfaces that were to represent metal. They were then fixed to temporary bases to ease the painting process.

After the painting of the trooper was completed, I started on the horse by cleaning and assembling the parts. Almost all parts could be assembled and glued at the beginning, except for the reins and the valise. During the assembly, some filler was required between the horse halves and the around the neck-to-body join.

Great care is demanded while attaching the scabbard straps as they first have to be bent into the correct shape before painting and gluing.

Step by Step

13

14

15

16

17

18

19

20

21

Step by Step

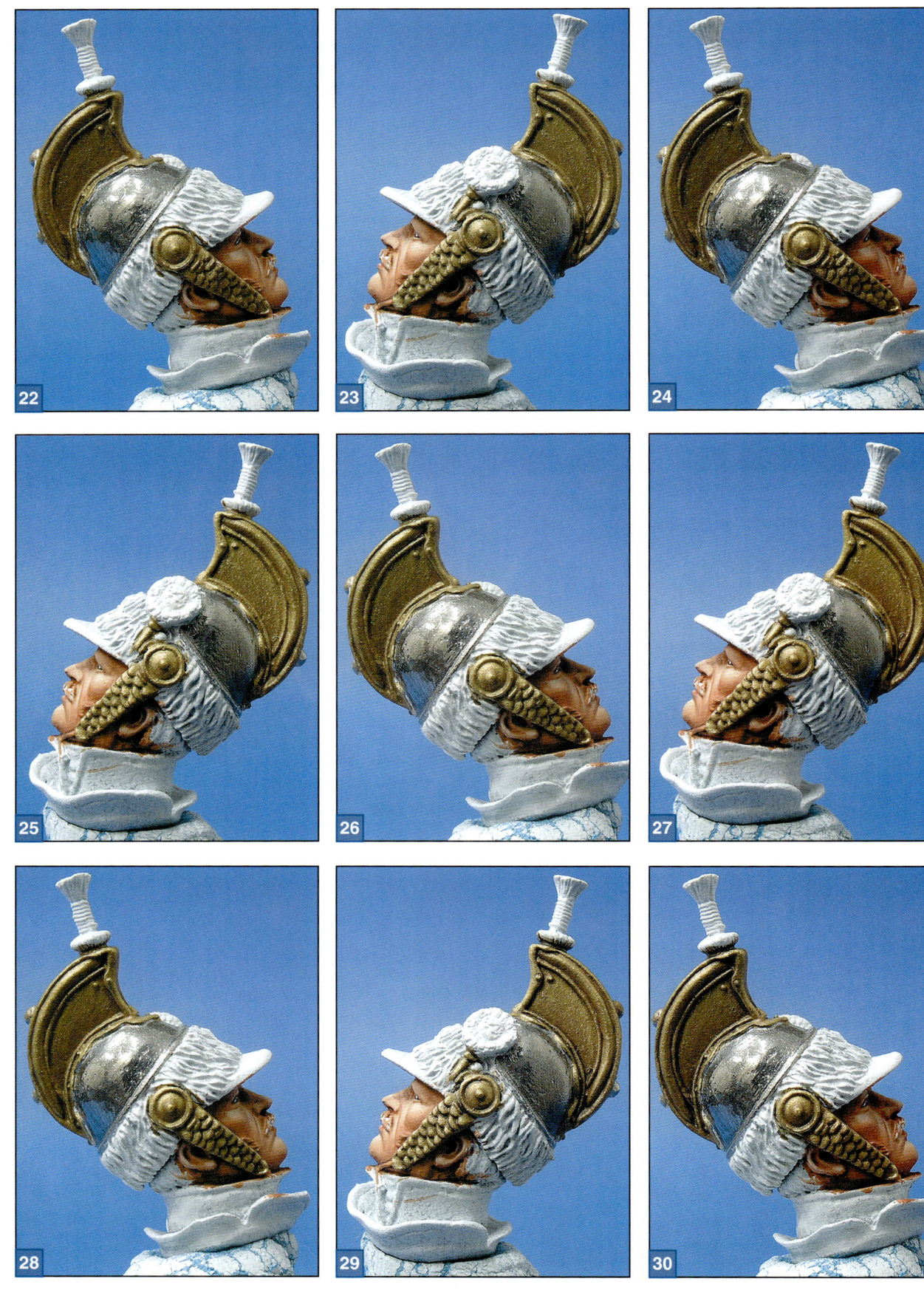

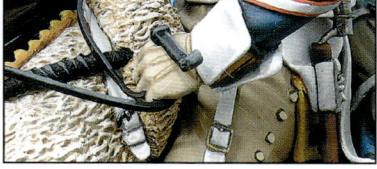

This view reveals how the rider holds the reins. Care is required to prevent breaking them, as they are fragile.

Close up of the sword's steel scabbard, and the regimental number on the shabraque, which was painted with a brush.

This view clearly shows the way the carbine hangs from its belt, and how the sword is held on the wrist.

The sculpting of horse's head is brilliant. A careful paint job will really make it stand out!

PAINTING

Skin

To paint the skin, I first mixed a base color of a reddish brown tone consisting of the following colors: 845 sunny skin tone, 921 English uniform, 908 carmine in respective proportions of 5:2:1 and acrylics. To achieve the required smooth surface over the whole of the skin surfaces previously primed with white (photo 1), we applied a first coat that was first highly diluted with water (photo 2) followed, at least 30 minutes later, with a second coat, although less diluted this time (photo 3). This is a necessary procedure for all acrylic colors, in order to obtain a smooth surface with no evident brushstrokes.

After the second coat of base color was dry, I began to highlight the face. Each highlighting step must be in a slightly lighter tone from the previous one, to get a very soft graduation between the tones. For the first highlight, I lightened the base color with 845 and applied a light coat over all the areas that needed to be highlighted (photo 4). After adding yet more 845 to the mixture used for the first highlight, I again applied it over the same areas although painting in smaller surfaces (photo 5). For the third highlight, I used even more 845 and painted it onto even smaller surfaces (photo 6). At this juncture, the face was already beginning to show its main volumes, while for the fourth highlight, I added even more 845 (photo 7). From this point, after the fourth highlight, I began to add 951 white instead of 845. In this way, I produced the fifth highlight shade (photo 8). For the sixth highlight

Rear view of the figure; especially note the set of the head and hair.

Step by Step

The helmet's fur turban was painted in a dark brown tone.

The helmet's horsehair mane has to be separately painted and then glued into position at the end.

After polishing the helmet's steel skull, I gave it a coat of smoke grey from Gunze.

shade, I added more white and applied it very carefully and only onto the extreme, highlight areas of the face (photo 9). The seventh, and final highlight is a pale pink tone and is used on the "corners" of the face, such as the cheekbones and chin (pic.10). For the shadows I used just three suitably diluted shades. The first shade was the base mixture with a little 921 and 908 added. Using this mixture, I applied it to those areas that do receive no light (photo 11). The second shadow shade is a bit darker than the previous one, and is a mixture of the first shadow with more 921 and 908 added. With the second shadow tone, I applied it to the same areas but on smaller surfaces (photo 12). The third and more intense shadow, consists of a mixture of equal amounts of 921 and 908, and is used primarily to define the face from the remaining elements of the head (photo 13). At this point the skin is done with just the eyes to be painted. These require extra attention, to make sure each one is centered properly. Finally, the lips were painted after adding some red to the bas color, and then highlighting with the addition of some white (photo 14).

Golds

For paint the gold-colored surfaces, I made a base mixture of 878 old gold, Andrea AC-gloss black, 941 burnt umber, 929 light brown, and a little 818 red leather, in proportions of around 6:2:2:1:1. As metal colors have a high transparency, I had to use three light coats of the base color. I began with the first coat, which did not cover very well (photos 15, 16). After 30 minutes, I gave it a second coat, taking care to apply it smoothly (photos 17, 18). As soon as this was dry, I applied a third coat, taking care to get complete coverage on all the surfaces (photos 19, 20).

Now it was time for the first highlight. After lightening the base color with some 878, I applied over all the raised areas (photos 21, 22). After adding even more gold to the previous mixture, I made the second highlight shade (photos 23, 24). For the third, and final highlight shade, I used a mixture of the base color, 878 old gold, and a little 953 flat yellow in a ratio of 1:3:1, and then painted all the corners to "lighten" them even more (photos 25, 26). The first shadow tone was slightly darker than the base color. To the base color, I added some black, a little 941, and a little 818, and was then highly diluted before applying it (photos 27, 28). Photos 29, 30 reveal that it is evident that it was the second and darker shadow, that of adding more black and 941 to the first shadow, which enhanced the sculpting of the figure. Following this procedure, and using these mixtures, I later painted the rest of the gold surfaces. To paint the rest of the parts of the figure and horse, I used a number of different color mixtures. These are presented below:

Blue Parts (Jacker-Shabraque-Valise)

Base: 965 Prussian blue + 950 black
Highlights: base + 965 + 951 white
Shadows: base + 950

Red Parts (Epaulettes-Jacket Cloth)

Base: 908 carmine
Highlights: base + 953 matt yellow + 845 sunny skin tone
Shadows: base + 926 red

Yellow Parts (Collar-Jacket Turnbacks)
Base: 953 matt yellow + AC-18 Andrea
Highlights: base + 953 + 951 white
Shadows: base + AC-18 Andrea

White Parts (Gloves-Sash-Belts)
Base: 951 white + 989 sky grey + 921 English uniform
Highlights: base + 951
Shadows: base + 989 + 921 + 950 black

Trousers
Base: 976 buff + 941 burnt umber + 845 sunny skin tone + 929 light brown
Highlights: base + 976 + 845 + 951
Shadows: base + 941 + 929

Black Parts (Boots-Horse Harness-Cartridge Pouch-Helmet Crest)
Base: 950 black + 989 sky grey + 921 English uniform
Highlights: base + 989 + 921 a
Shadows: base + 950

Cuirass Straps
Base: 941 burnt umber
Highlights: base + 929 light brown
Shadows: base + 950 black

Helmet Fur-Horsehair Mane and Tail
Base: 950 black + 989 sky grey + 984 matt brown
Highlights: base + 984 + 989(dry brush)
Shadows: 950 (wash)

Harness Fur
Base: 951 white + 953 matt yellow + 929 light brown
Highlights: base + 951(dry brush)
Shadows: base + 929 + 941(wash)

Cloth Bag Blanket
Base: 989 sky grey + 992 neutral grey + 921 English uniform
Highlights: base + 989 + 951 white
Shadows: base + 992 + 921

Gunstock
Base: 875 beige brown + 908 carmine + 950 black
Highlights: base + 875 + 845 sunny skin tone
Shadows: base + 984 matt brown + 950

Horse Hide
Base: 984 matt brown + 818 red leather + 950 black + 908 carmine
Highlights: base + 818 + 929 light brown

The upper part of horse's head, showing the white flash.

Shadows: base + 950

As soon as the hide had been painted, I used a thin coat of burnt umber oil paint, which was lightly dabbed on with a soft cloth. This action gives depth to the colors, and the hair obtains a characteristic shine.

BASE
Ground
Base: 873 US field drab
Highlights: base + 845 sunny skin tone + 953 matt yellow (dry brush)
Shadows: base + 941 burnt umber + 950(wash)

Rock
Base: 992 neutral grey + 921 English uniform
Highlights: base + 989 sky grey + 951 white (dry brush)
Shadows: base + 950 (wash)

After completing the painting of the different parts, I assembled the rider, and then attached him onto the horse, which was already secured to the base.

At the earliest cleaning stage, I drilled holes and inserted metal pins into all the heavier parts to better secure them.

EPILOGUE
Every large-scale piece demands many hours of work because of the large number of parts that make up the model. This is especially so when making a mounted model, like the Andrea Cuirassier. The difficult part is to decide what parts should be

Step by Step

Seen here is the valise with the regimental number on each end.

Below, the shoulder belt for the carbine swivel, and a second belt for the cartridge box.

Looking at the elements of the base, the position of the horse, and the added details, such as tree stumps.

The view of the completed model from the front is really impressive.

attached prior to, or after painting, so that they don't get in the way during any subsequent painting. This Andrea kit demanded almost two months work (I had nothing else on the go at the same time!) before it could be placed in the showcase. The proper planning of each work stage is essential, even before cleaning the parts. So, there's no doubt, experience is needed which is why these types of figures are not recommended for beginners, maybe not even for intermediate skill modelers, even if they could accept the high cost that, in some cases, might be prohibitive.

Despite this, a mounted figure, especially in 90 mm scale is always impressive.

SS Standartenführer

While I personally paint very few stock figures, and even less busts, my friend's love for German uniforms led to this project. It didn't take him long to decide that he wanted one and he asked me to paint it for him. I'm happy that he did. Painting this bust was a delightful experience because of its exquisite sculpting and the final overall result.

STEPHEN MALLIA

> 200 mm
> SS Standartenführer: Pegaso (200-003)
> White metal
> Acrylic paints: Vallejo and Andrea
> Primer: Citadel's Skull White

The figure is cast in white metal and is to Pegaso's usual high standard. Mould lines were minimal and, in some areas, almost invisible. There are just a few parts to assemble - hat, bust and two crosses - so one can really concentrate on the actual painting. The cleaning up of the figure, which took very little time, was done using some needle files, sandpaper and, finally, some fine steel wool for polishing the parts. Three holes were drilled; the first two would, with the help of small brass rods, reinforce the joint at the top of the head to the bottom of the hat. The other would accommodate the metal pin that would go into the base.

The first step in the painting process was a coat of primer. I use a spray can of Citadel's Skull White for this. Over the years, I've used several primers, but I find this to be one of the best. The trick with it is to spray from a little distance and go for one or two coats. If you spray too close, the paint covers very thick with obvious results. This primer coat dries rather quickly, but I never take chances and leave it overnight to give it time to really cure.

The painting itself began with the eyes; when painting a full figure the face is always the point of focus. With busts, on the other hand, which are practically only a face, the eyes take the dominant role and special care needs to be taken to ensure these are as natural as possible and all the minute details have to be present. To achieve this, I refer to magazines that have many close-up shots of faces - fashion, cosmetics, hair, etc., which will provide a lot of details of these areas.

For this subject, I opted for blue eyes as I thought it was the most suitable color. I will provide a color chart at the end for the mixtures used, but first I will go through my techniques. I won't just say that the dilution rates I use are standard, because they obviously aren't. For example, for the base coat I use a 1:1 ratio. In this case, whilst the paint is not thick enough to cover any detail, it still retains its covering power, and I always let the paint dry before applying the next coat.

For the highlights, the paint to water ratio is approximately 1:4 or even 1:5, I use these ratios just for painting busts, for smaller faces I use a higher ratio. I try not to overload the brush with paint, although if I do have too much paint, I wipe the excess on a piece of tissue.

With each highlight layer (usually 3) I might add water to keep the dilution consistent. With the highlights done, it's time to do the shadows. With small-scale figures, the shadows and highlights are more like an optical illusion (or make up); on busts they are somewhat more natural. A stark contrast is needed on small-scale figures to create such optical illusions; whilst on large-scale busts the contrast is more subtle and natural.

My dilution ratios for shadows are always higher than those for the highlights, usually 1:8 – 1:10. When applying them, extra care needs to be taken, as the paint is so thin it will run wild if the brush is overloaded. The primary shadows were mostly done in two stages, with one slightly darker than the other. The beard area was applied using controlled washes and any highlights needed in this area were done using the base

color. The main uniform areas were basically painted in the same way, but using a slightly larger brush (No.2).

The hat and crosses were attached after all the painting was finished and, when everything was dry, the bust was attached to its base. As an adhesive, two-part epoxy glue was used throughout.

And Voila! ... Another German subject for my friend's collection. This really was an enjoyable experience and I can strongly recommend this figure.

The colors used throughout for the project came from the Vallejo and Andrea ranges. Some gold printers' ink was used for the shoulder rank pips. I used Winsor & Newton Series 7 brushes throughout.

The paint mixtures used are as follows:
(AV: Vallejo, AC: Andrea)

FLESH
Base: AV845 + AV909 + AC-2 + AC-14
Highlight 1: base + AV845 + AV928
Highlight 2: highlight + AV928
Shadow 1: base + AC-14 + AC-2
Shadow 2: AV909 + AC-26

BEARD AREA
Washes of base + AV994 + AC-26

UNIFORM JACKET
Base: AC1 + AV994 + AV886
Highlight 1: base + AV886
Highlight 2: AV886
Shadow 1: base + AC-26
Shadow 2: more AC-26

After all the highlights and shadows were applied, a highly diluted wash of the base color was applied to assist in the soft transition of the colors.

HAT
I tried to slightly vary the colors between the hat and the uniform while, in the meantime, retaining the same tones. By altering the percentage of one color and adding more of another you can achieve a different shade of the same color. The peak was given a couple of coats of gloss varnish. Below is the mixtures used.

Base: AC1 + AV994 + AC-59
Highlight 1: base + AC-59
Highlight 2: AC-59
Shadows 1: base + AV994
Shadow 2: shadow 1 + AC-26

The photos show areas in close-up. The shoulder rank decorations have very little silver paint in them, they were painted using greys and whites and the same goes for the buttons. For the shoulder decorations, I predominantly made use of the color AC-60 while AC-59 mixed with black and AC-60 was used for the buttons.

Step by Step

SS PANZERGRENADIER 1945
"Painting Italian camouflage"

TEXT-PHOTOGRAPHS: JAUME ORTIZ FORNS
UNIFORMOLOGY NOTES: DANIEL ALFONSEA

Our subject figure is kit No: AM35005 from the Italian firm of Alexander Miniatures. It portrays a late-war SS Grenadier on the Eastern Front. The figure is impeccably produced in resin, and combines an appealing pose with a very high degree of detail. Two head options with different headdresses are included in the kit, helmet with camouflage cover or a fur hat.

UNIFORMOLOGY NOTES

The most remarkable element of this figure is the Waffen-SS-style parka in the Italian camouflage pattern. This organization is often credited with the development of the anorak/parka as a military garment – at least, they were among the first to use what is now regarded as a common piece of equipment; it was already being worn during experimental trials in Norway and Finland in 1940.

Waffen-SS troops were issued with the first model of fur-lined parka during the winter of 1942-43, and it featured quite prominently during the Battle of Kharkov in March 1943; in fact, the garment is commonly associated with this engagement, it being so commonplace in campaign photos that it is frequently referred to as the "Kharkov Parka." This first model was pull-over style, made in fur-lined mouse grey or field grey cloth; these two latter features were retained for the next model, which appeared in 1944, and had a full button-up front, this being more practical for accessibility to underclothes and ventilation. There was also some variation in pocket style and other minor details. Different kinds of animal fur was used, white fleece and rabbit being the most usual, but other, more luxurious skins are occasionally found, because of the confiscation of civilian property. Mismatched furs, both in color and in quality, could also occur on the same garment.

This item of clothing was considered to be a protective garment, adequate for the more extreme sub-zero environments, hence it was intended to be restricted to the Eastern front. The widespread reversible two-piece uniform was deemed sufficient or most other environments.

The second model parka was also manufactured from Italian camouflage material, apparently very late in the war. Not much is known of this particular variant, but its wartime use is confirmed by contemporary photographs. This gives the modeller the chance of attempting a more unusual paint scheme for the figure, as already suggested on the box-art.

Under the parka the soldier wears his regular Feldgrau uniform, M1943 pattern, in this instance combined with the archetypical jackboots, which were never completely superseded by the more economical

Different views of the completed figure, showing both the heads included with the kit. The camouflaged helmet cover was painted following the same techniques detailed in the main text, obviously addressing to the need of representing a different pattern, in this case the Oak-Leaf A (Spring side out).

laced short boots and canvas leggings. The Stg 44 assault rifle is an appropriate weapon for the late war image, as is the ubiquitous Panzerfaust 60.

PAINTING CAMOUFLAGES

When tackling the painting of scale figures in camouflage uniforms, a number of factors will have to take into account that will greatly influence the final result. The difference between a camouflage pattern represented in a realistic form, and a number of haphazardly applied color blotches on a base color will depend on the skill of the painter.

• **Sources:** It is incontestable that, if one wishes to obtain good results when painting scale camouflage, one first has to gain a thorough knowledge of the chosen pattern. If aiming for an identifiable pattern, you should try to make it as close to the original as possible; if, for some reason, this is not possible, the "style" should, at least, be imitated. To this end, it is imperative to refer to good graphic sources, to be able copy the actual pattern.

In this particular case, the Italian camouflage pattern has a bluish-green background, over which are found large, irregular, undulating red brown splotches, and similarly-shaped smaller ochre splotches, always impressed over the larger ones. This splotch pattern is repeated and this must be evident on the uniform to be painted.

It must also be clearly understand where the splotch design is interrupted. Usually, an item of uniform is made up of several pieces of cloth cut to a pattern and then sewn together. The seams will separate the pattern, which will then begin at a different point, and may even be in a different

Step by Step

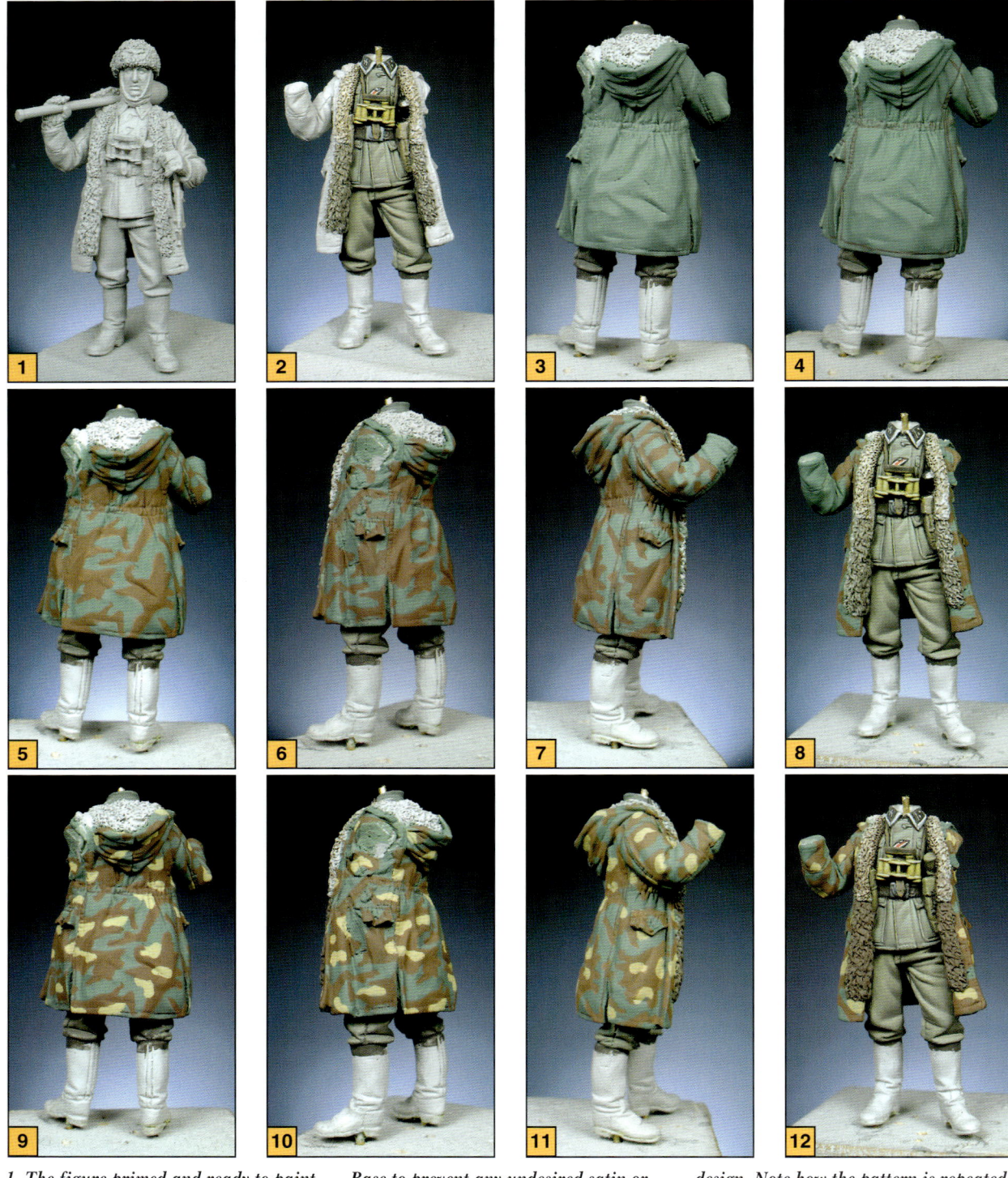

1. The figure primed and ready to paint with the Tamiya primer I always use. The figure has been fixed to a temporary base for comfortable handling.
2. I began with those items of uniform in field grey, including the collar and other insignia details, because the camouflaged parka is worn over them, and it is easier to do it in this order.
3. The camouflage base color on the parka. I mixed it with some Tamiya Flat Base to prevent any undesired satin or gloss appearance. At this stage, the left arm has not been glued on, as it would make it that much harder to paint the surrounding areas.
4. I outlined every seam on the parka with dark brown; this helped to make me aware of those points where the camouflage pattern is interrupted.
5-8. Painting the brown splotches. While doing this, I closely followed the actual design. Note how the pattern is repeated. In the more hidden areas, or where access is difficult, it is impossible to exactly replicate the actual pattern, although I did maintain the "style."
9-12. Painting the yellowish-ochre splotches. Again, the design is repeated. These splotches always tend towards the brown ones. Note how I painted the pattern with a different orientation on several areas.

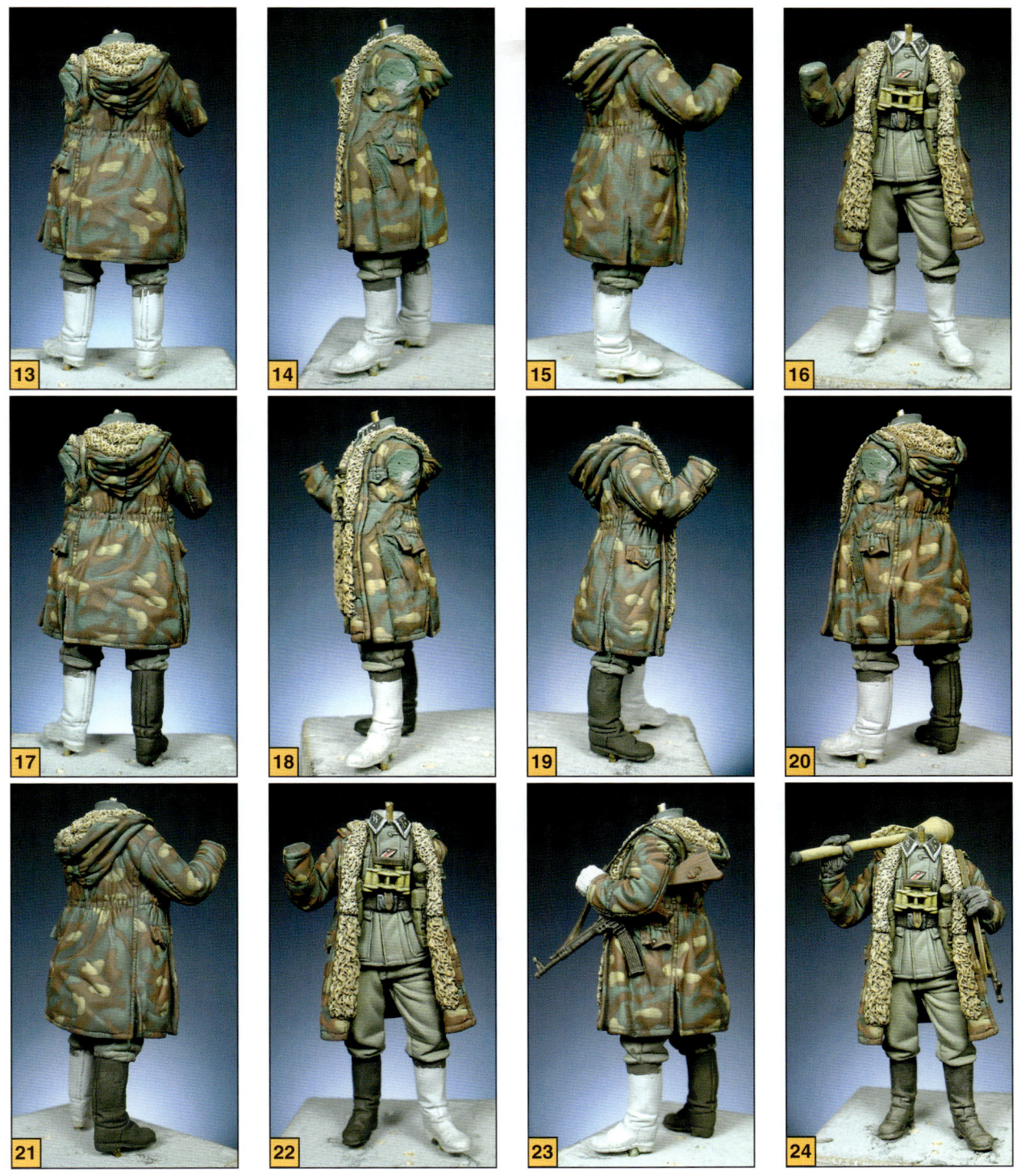

13-16. I shadowed the whole garment with highly diluted German camouflage black brown 822 washes. It is preferable to give it three highly diluted washes than a single, thicker one, as doing it with the thicker wash may overshadow the design. These washes, in addition to unifying all the camouflage colors also contribute to a realistic appearance.
17-22. The completed camouflage pattern, including highlighting. Each color was individually addressed, trying to give depth to every fold and shape while, at the same time, taking care not to lose the pattern's identity. Note how underlined seams, pockets, etc, contribute to a pleasing impression of depth.
23. Once I had finished the left side area, I glued on the left arm, complete with weapon. I then painted the left sleeve, following the previous procedure. The rifle sling was made from paper, set to shape with Super Glue and then adapted to the shape of the figure.
24. The Panzerfaust, complete with hand. This anti-tank weapon was painted in ochre tones; I imitated the chipped paint with dark brown, using a stippling action.

Step by Step

orientation. Pay close attention to these details and the camouflage you are simulating will be more realistic and eye-catching.

• **Color:** Again, reference sources are paramount. The colors of a given camouflage pattern may very well vary from one garment to another, and even on the same one. The color range applicable for the selected uniform must be identified and then portrayed as closely as possible.

It must be taken into account that the surface to be worked on is 35 times smaller than the actual one, so the colors must be darkened to compensate for the "scale factor."

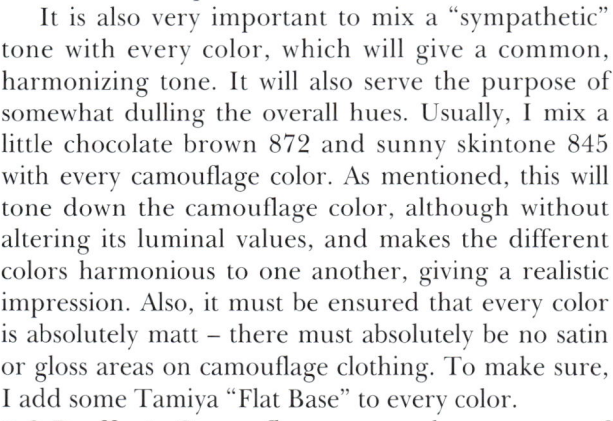

The finished figure.

It is also very important to mix a "sympathetic" tone with every color, which will give a common, harmonizing tone. It will also serve the purpose of somewhat dulling the overall hues. Usually, I mix a little chocolate brown 872 and sunny skintone 845 with every camouflage color. As mentioned, this will tone down the camouflage color, although without altering its luminal values, and makes the different colors harmonious to one another, giving a realistic impression. Also, it must be ensured that every color is absolutely matt – there must absolutely be no satin or gloss areas on camouflage clothing. To make sure, I add some Tamiya "Flat Base" to every color.

• **3-D effect:** Camouflage serves the purpose of integrating the garment with the background, and at the same time distorting the wearer's shape and outline.

When painting camouflage on a figure's clothing, the result tends to have a "flat" appearance. The pattern somewhat blurs the folds and other details, that do not stand out. To counteract this, the camouflaged uniform has to be shaded and highlighted, in the same as with a solid color garment, to regain the desired depth to the sculpted details. One needs to be very careful at this point – too much shadowing and highlighting may "denaturalize" the pattern, making it confusing or even unrecognizable.

Generally, I apply a general shadowing using dark brown highly diluted washes over the whole of the pattern; later, I concentrate, with equally thinned pure black washes, on the deepest creases and any areas that are more hidden from the light source.

I then individually highlight every spot of color in the appropriate areas using the original tones. Finally, I add some Sunny skintone 845 to every color on the most prominent zones.

The careful outlining of seams, and any parts that stand out from their surrounding surfaces, will also pay dividends.

COLOR CHART

Italian Camouflage:

	BASE COLOR *	HIGHLIGHTS
Green	olive grey 888 + blue green 808 (70/30%)	Adding sunny skintone 845
Red Brown	matt brown 984 + German cam. black brown 984 (60/40%)	Adding mahogany brown 846
Yellow Ochre	desert yellow 977 + chocolate brown 872 (80/20%)	Adding more desert yellow

*A little chocolate brown and sunny skintone was mixed with each color.

Field Grey clothing:

	BASE COLOR	HIGHLIGHTS	SHADOWS
German Jacket	field grey 830	Adding sunny skintone 845	Adding matt black
Trousers	German field grey 830	Adding green sky 974	Adding matt black

2nd Ranger Battalion
Omaha Beach, Normandy, 6th June 1944

Seven kilometers west of "Omaha" beach, 255 men from the 2nd Rangers Battalion, landed on the lower part of Cape Hawk.

CHRISTOS STAMATOPOULOS

54 mm
Sergeant 2nd US Rangers, Normandy, 6th June 1944: Soldiers (SF-01)
Acrylic colors: Vallejo Oil colors: Winsor & Newton Accessories: Verlinden

The Allies believed that on the top of the cliffs was situated a very dangerous artillery unit. It was supposed to consist of six 155 mm guns with an effective range of 24 km. After engaging in a tough battle with the German Army's 716th Infantry Regiment, the US Rangers reached the top and took many prisoners. However, no guns were discovered, just bases with telegraph poles! The Allies later found the mystery guns farther inland. The Rangers managed to hold their position for two days, but at a cost of 138 casualties.

I faced no difficulties during the assembly of the figure, so I shall move on to priming and painting.

PAINTING

Face (with oils)
Undercoat: 955 flat flesh
Base: yellow ochre + burnt sienna
Highlights: titanium white
Shadows: Burnt umber, burnt sienna

Trousers
Base: 890 reflective green
Highlights: base + 917 beige
Shadows: base + 921 English Uniform

Leggings
Base: 924 Russian uniform
Highlights: base + 917 beige
Shadows: 924 + 950 black (2%)

Rucksack-Canteen (Case)-Cartridges (Cases)-Straps
Base: 914 olive green + 5% 967 olive green
Highlights: base + 917 beige
Shadows: base + 921 English uniform

The sculpting of the figure is excellent, making it very helpful for the painter.

The bunker was painted in gray tones and then followed with a wash of dark gray and black.

The figure's pose is realistic and the fine detail on the webbing is very good.

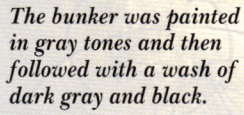

Thompson Machine Gun
Metal Parts: gunmetal + black (washes with oil paint)
Wooden Parts: 818 red leather + 941 burnt umber (plus washes with burnt umber oil paint)

Boots
941 burnt umber + 5% 818 red leather

Helmet
896 extra dark green

BASE
The figure's base was built by John Karousis. The upper part of the gun pit is from the Verlinden range, while the rest was made of wood, plaster and wire on some points to recreate the concrete's wire reinforcement.

PAINTING THE BASE
I used sand tones, while the gun pit was painted in gray and black.

SS Sturmbanfuhrer of Artillery

2nd SS Panzer Division
The Officer Who Watched the Panzers Pass By…

DIEGO RUINA
PHOTOGRAPHS:
PEGASO STUDIO

90 mm
SS Sturmbanfuhrer of Artillery, 2nd SS Panzer Division "Das Reich," France 1944: Pegaso Models, "Elite Series" (90-041)
Acrylic colors: Vallejo, Andrea
Enamel varnish: Testors

Autumn, 1944… the German officer, accompanied by his faithful companion, watches with embarrassment — it is true — as the panzers pass before him heading for the front. The last armor reserves need to get to the battle in order to stop the Allies advancing. The news is not good. He lights a cigarette and thinks back to the good old days when, just a few short years ago, he stood on the same spot as a conqueror and not as a defender…

From this particular angle both the German officer and his dog are seen to very good effect. Look closely at the weathering of his boots and greatcoat and the motion of the animal. Special care was taken painting the dog's snout to attain this particular effect.

A head-on view of the small vignette in which all the significant parts are prominent: the German officer, the dog and the lamppost with the road signs; special care was given to the representation of the muddy ground.

Pegaso's 90mm white metal figure represents a German officer who could have fought at innumerable places, on different fronts and under various scenarios, from Stalingrad to France, before or after the Allied invasion of Normandy.

I selected the latter scenario, that is three months after the Allies had landed in Normandy when, at the end of the summer, large numbers of German reinforcements passed through France – which had already flooded because of the heavy rains – heading from south, centre and east to the north-west, in a hopeless effort to contain the advancing Allied forces.

It is here, behind the front line, near one of the many country villages, at the side of a muddy country road ploughed up by the tracks of the heavy panzers, that a German officer watches with embarrassment as one of the many armor convoys head north.

PREPARATION AND CONSTRUCTION

Preparing to assemble the figure was not particularly difficult, to begin all the mould lines were removed with a sharp blade and a fine file and, following that, the complete figure was polished with a soft wire brush in a power tool. At this point, my first priority was to dry-fit the figure's body and the great coat, which consists of two parts and has to be glued onto the figure after, not only the rest of the uniform but also the inner part of the coat itself has been painted. Fortunately, the parts fit was excellent and did not require any use of putty filler, as it corresponded exactly with the leather.

Despite the excellent fit, in order to make the figure as stable as possible, I drilled holes and inserted two pins in the two halves of the greatcoat, which helped me with their correct alignment. Also, drilling and inserting large pins in the bottom of the figure's feet of such a large figure is crucial. The dog also required a small amount of putty to fill the joints. Moreover, for the same reasons mentioned above, I inserted two small pins in the dog's legs. After again test-fitting the figure's main parts, I sprayed it with several coats of grey primer.

After I had finished the preparation and assembly of the figure on the one hand, and had chosen the appropriate scenario on the other, I drilled the requisite holes in the base and created the terrain with epoxy putty, which I shaped with my hands while it was still damp. I also needed a length of wood for the lamppost, plasticard for the road signs and some brass wire to represent the metal parts of the lamppost. In the end, though, I had to cut it down to just above the figure's head, as I had made it too tall for the vignette.

To sand smooth parts of the figure, I used various degrees of sandpaper along with a small motor-tool wire brush. To correctly represent the officer's belt, I used some rings from an old resin parts kit for a 1:15 Tiger that, although they are slightly too large, are, fortunately, hardly noticeable.

PAINTING

As usual, I began the painting of the figure with the face, starting with the eyes and then shifting them slightly to the left. Next, I made the skin color in a tone not too dark, with a hint of a two-day beard. All the painting was done using Vallejo acrylic colors, starting with the dark tones and gradually lightening them up.

After that I dealt with the uniform, which was also painted with acrylics – this time from the Andrea range, but using the same technique. After applying a very dark base made of aviation green, black, flesh (carne) and a little maroon, I applied the first highlights by lightening the base color with green and flesh (carne) and then completed the final highlights with flesh and beige from the Andrea range for the very last details.

If you want to avoid mistakes with the color shades, it is important to have a photo of a well-preserved uniform– or at least a good copy showing the original colors. Always remember that, although you have to simulate the right shades, you don't have to worry about the exact color mixtures, as different effects of light and shadow, other painting effects and weathering render any effort to represent the perfect color tone almost useless. It is best to say that, in most cases, the actual colors should be somewhere between the light and the dark shades; shadow should correspond to a darker tone, whereas light to a lighter one, it that should not turn the color towards either the warm or the cold shades.

The tunic and trousers of the uniform are the same color – just a light wash with blue for the first and with brown for the latter has slightly differentiated the shade of the base color.

I then moved onto the boots and belt and painted them with a warmer shade of black using Vallejo acrylics, which are slightly more translucent in comparison to the Andrea ones. I applied a base of black lightened with a little red, and then dry brushed them with ochre and beige, so that I could highlight the edges and simulate some slight weathering.

There are a number of fine details that can really make the difference: for example, the cigarette in the officer's right hand, the belt buckle, the pistol holster, the "texture" of the leather greatcoat, as well as the torn proclamation poster and the rusted pieces of iron on the lamppost.

The collar, the cap and the various finishes were all painted with acrylics and, finally, the buttons, buckles and other metal parts were painted with acrylic silver over Vallejo black, the reflections of which were emphasised with silver printers' ink.

One of the most significant parts of the whole uniform, not only because of its outstanding sculpting of its shape and dimensions is, for sure, the black leather greatcoat. In essence, the painting procedure was the same as for the boots; however, it was adapted for covering a much larger surface. First, I painted the inner areas with black and then highlighted them, before gluing the two parts of the coat to the figure and then completing the painting procedure.

The next job was to apply a base of opaque Vallejo black, which was highlighted after adding a little red to the mixture and applying two or three coats to get those brownish shades. If you want to avoid a dark brown shade, make sure that the highlights are moderate and light, so that they just slightly emphasise the volume of the figure. The actual highlights were done after adding a little golden flesh (carne dorata) to the mixture and then applying a wash on the highlighted areas, concentrating on just some of the edges and the more weathered belts.

On the more highlighted and weathered parts, I applied little touches of highly diluted beige, but only on some edges and creases. I continued accentuate the recesses with pure black. I continued adding some highlights and weathering to refine the painting of the figure.

I completed the painting process by painting the buttons and epaulets. Finally, I painted the pistol holster, which features some nice fine detail, in the same way as the boots and greatcoat,

THE DOG

In order to paint the animal's coat correctly, it is important to have a good photograph of one – in this case a German Shepherd. Disregarding the colors, the painting technique for an animals' coat is the same for all of them: the colors must be painted in very fine, close lines. We should not take into account just the highlights and shadows, but also the different shades of the animal's hair.

First, I applied a base for each basic color, I painted the animal's back black, then its body with light brown mixed with a little red – some areas were lighter, others a little darker – and I tried to define the strips of colors with small parallel lines without clear boundaries.

The next step was to highlight the various shades, always by painting small lines and, in some areas, by carefully blending the colors so that no clear distinction between the shades can be seen.

Particular care was given to the animal's snout, its nose and eyes, these should be very well defined as well as accurate – especially the eyes as these should appear perfectly lucid.

After I had finished with the animal's coat, I painted its leash with a leather color and then took care of the buckle and other small details.

THE GROUNDWORK

I wanted to give the impression of muddy ground after heavy rain, where the surface water still runs in the grooves made by the panzers' tracks.

The base colors for the groundwork consists of shades of brown, lightened with a little ochre and flesh (carne), which I gradually treated with numerous washes of black and green, especially around the lamppost. A final touch of dry brushing using various shades of beige completes the

A close-up view of the German Shepherd. Apart from the excellent overall detail, the figure of the dog is really accentuated by the painting procedure described in the text. The rear of the greatcoat can also be seen to good effect.

painting of the ground.

The lamppost is made of actual wood and this is the reason it absorbed so much paint. Using the wash technique, in this case many coats of it because of the wood's absorbency, with black, brown and beige colors and a trace of green. This was done in a non-homogenous way to achieve a typical drab greenish shade of old lampposts that have long been exposed to the weather. After these washes had completely dried, it was time for the gradual application of dry brushing effects using beige and then white, which gave the lamppost both depth and volume. The road signs are made of plasticard cut and then torn with a sharp blade. After gluing them to the lamppost, I painted them black and, finally, I washed and dry brushed them in order to give them a heavily weathered look. The lettering on them was quickly made with a brush.

The torn proclamation poster, it can be either on the lamppost or on the ground, was made from a piece of paper moistened with water and Vinavil and then positioned where I wanted it and allowed to dry. Next, it received some washes of black, brown and green colors, while the print on it was painted black. Afterwards, I tore it with a blade in order to simulate damage due to the awful weather conditions.

The water effect was created with thick Vinavil, painted with acrylic colors and then laid aside to dry. After it was completely dry, I gave the base and the lower part of the lamppost lots of coats of transparent Testors enamel colors in order to represent the moisture and the water after the rain. Finally, I positioned the figure and the dog on the base and then I glued them in place with epoxy glue, thus making sure everything was really secure!

After the glue had dried, I simulated the dust and dirt on the German officer's greatcoat and boots, as well as on the dog's legs with a brown, black and ochre wash. Keeping the effect to a minimum, as I wanted to show that he had been in the fields for just a little although, in this muddy terrain, it is inevitable that usual signs of mud should be present.

A few touches of gloss varnish here and there on the lower parts of the boots and the capote to represent the still wet mud completed the figure.